T0069017

Doing

THE FRENCH LIST

www.bibliofrance.in

The work is published with the support of the
Publication Assistance Programmes of the Institut français

Seagull Books, 2020

Originally published as *Que faire?* by Jean-Luc Nancy
© Éditions Galilée, 2016

First published in English translation by Seagull Books, 2020

English translation of *Doing* © Charlotte Mandell, 2020

English translation of 'A Coming Without Past or Future'
© Nikolaas Deketelaere and Marie Chabbert, 2020

ISBN 978 0 8574 2 784 7

British Library Cataloguing-in-Publication Data
A catalogue record for this book is available from the British Library

Typeset by Seagull Books, Calcutta, India
Printed and bound by Versa Press, East Peoria, Illinois, USA

Doing

JEAN-LUC NANCY

TRANSLATED BY CHARLOTTE MANDELL

Followed by
'A Coming Without Past or Future'

TRANSLATED BY
NIKOLAAS DEKETELAERE AND MARIE CHABBERT

LONDON NEW YORK CALCUTTA

CONTENTS

A NOTE ON THE TRANSLATION

The French title of this book is *Que faire?*, which brings to mind Lenin's epochal text *Chto Delat?*, translated into English as *What Is to Be Done*. Since the passive form of the verb isn't in keeping with Jean-Luc Nancy's use of *faire*, and since a literal translation of *Que faire?* like *What to Do?* sounds a bit foreign to a native English speaker (we usually say What should do we do?, or What can we do?), after consulting with the author, we agreed that *Doing* would be a good title for the English publication of the book, especially since it's in keeping with several other books I've translated by Jean-Luc Nancy, *Coming* and *Listening*.

The French verb *faire* can be translated as both 'do' and 'make'; it is therefore one of the most widely used verbs in the language. Some examples of French phrases using the word: *faire l'amour* [to make love], *faire un rêve* [to have a dream], *s'en faire* [to worry], *se faire à* [to get used to], *faire un enfant* [to have a child], *faire de l'argent* [to make money], *faire du travail* [to do work], *faire ses études* [to do one's studies] ... The uses of *faire* in French are myriad and multiform; the English verb 'do' doesn't really do justice to *faire*, but we'll have to make do with it for now ...

Charlotte Mandell

BRIEF ACTIVIST PREAMBLE

Unemployment (as if 'full-time employment' were the only ideal), mass unemployment (as if a single unemployed person weren't already burdened with a mass of anxiety), winning or losing (as if one could do only the one or other), the growing gap between rich and poor (as if this gap weren't carved out by the former at the expense of the latter), war and terrorism (as if terror hadn't risen up to us from the depths of our comfortable peace), technological and natural catastrophes (as if you could still tell the difference), dismantling of public services (as if 'services' were not an essential commodity), clash of civilizations (as if there weren't one single civilization, soaked in its own violence), collapse of values (as if there were any other kind than the sort that could be converted into money), murderous religions (as if murder weren't already ritual), corrupt politics (as if they weren't already ruptured [*rompue, corrompue*]), rousing editorials in favour of a rediscovered democracy (as if it had ever been found), petitions for solidarity, fraternity, justice (as if it were a matter of slogans) . . .

Let's stop these clichés: Hasn't everything already been whisked away without a trace (one more cliché . . .)?

So, we can begin.

But don't be content with reading. Do something.

INTRODUCTION

'In a time when all humanity tends to be lost': these words appear unexpectedly from an article devoted to a poet, in a poetry journal published in early December 2015.[1] By taking the time to leaf through journals and magazines of the present moment, I could soon gather a large collection of the same sort. I think irresistibly of Freud, who, about 85 years ago, wrote that humanity now had the means to destroy itself. The feeling of a disaster persists and progresses—it is even the only progress we seem to be making, we weary pedestrians on a path that seems to be losing itself in an undergrowth that is stifling history.

What is barely whispering behind this long *lamento* drawn out on a 'soiled world' [*monde immonde*] (trite expression for 30 years now) is the question 'What to do?' Only the question, since we no longer think of the slightest actual answer, despite the fact that papers of all kinds overflow with informed analyses and shrewd advice. The height of our confusion is that we don't even dare ask the question any more. Everything is undone, everything is perhaps remade entirely differently, remotely, but nothing allows us—'us' the latecomers as Nietzsche said, 'us' we folk of the evening, we Westerners—to ask a question whose very concept escapes us: the

1 Jean-Paul Auxeméry in *Po&sie* 152 (November 2015): 60.

question of an action directed to a precise goal with controlled means.

The deterioration of the State and political parties, or more generally of the forces working to seize hold of them, their domination by economic and technological powers, the global remodelling of roles, models, relationships keep us from seeing reference points for action. Gone are the days when class or generational movements, movements of popular, national, cultural liberation, knew on what to base their plans, where to focus their goals, how to endow themselves with power. The most 'radical' (what a dusty word!) rebellions are the most idealistic and least realistic; the most demanding summons is the dreamiest.

Waves of fanatical violence are greeted with heroic and virtuosic stances in which it is easy to see that no one believes, not even those who adopt them.

2

Surely it's not by chance if already, while waiting for Godot, we wondered 'What can we do?' A little later on, with Godard, a girl intoned: 'What can I do? I don't know what to do!' Godot, the one who does not arrive; Godard, the one who says 'farewell to language'. These will become our inaugural mottos when Europe has been ruined and carried off on a new course of world affairs. When the word 'communism' has been left by the wayside with all its explosive charge defused. When Europe has been transformed into an ironic market community. When energy needs require conflicts. When colonial liberations have been monopolized by dictators and appropriated by former colonial powers. When imperialism is reorganized and reterritorialized while the old West struggles to keep its place. When all our ideas of history, the human and sense have themselves been summoned before the court of the rational.

There's nothing surprising about this, that 'doing'—action, production, setting underway or performing—became uncertain on its own. 'Realization' has become so problematic that it may have seemed to some that reality itself were lacking, or that they could discern only the slightest relationship between object and calculating subject. Reality, however, cannot disappear, nor vanish into images. On the contrary, it is reality that is being valued today. It is being valued with a value that no evaluation can foresee.

We should know that 'any theoretical powerlessness in itself testifies to a real perception: the grasp of a radical *beginning*, a new form of political organization and existence, irreducible to any theoretical reduction of foundation or deduction, the grasp of an irreversible fact of history.'

These lines of Althusser[2] bear a few marks of the time. The metaphysics of the 'beginning' and the linked metaphysics of 'radicality' could be threatening. But the important thing is the keen awareness of testimony a powerlessness bears: something resists already-formed understandings. A fact clashes with the ideas

---

2 Louis Althusser, *Politique et histoire de Machiavel à Marx* (*1955–1972*) (Paris: Seuil, 2006), pp. 247–8 (with thanks to Françoise Metz).

of doing. It resists because it resists, without yet knowing in whose name. As Alexander Garcia Düttman writes: 'Resistance always also amounts to an intractable tautology. It just resists.'[3]

3

What to do? It seems to me that there are, without any hesitation, two answers that seem obvious and that complement each other. One: We must change the question. Two: We are already doing it.

Yes, doing it. In this very place. By writing. Not by writing a speech; rather, it is the practice of working out thought that is action, that is even the most urgent action we need—an action, moreover, that is already happening, being done in many places, in many writings, many voices.

I'm not calling for us to oppose the lost and already disheartened 'What to do?' as if I were trying to build up troop morale. No, I'm simply saying that we are already doing. Not that it's all done, of course—when it's done, it's over, we know that. But it's in the process of being done, without a doubt. (Not even mentioning all the actions, initiatives, fights, engagements great and small that are

---

3 'No matter how much it may be embedded in a discourse of explanation and justification, no matter how reasonable and how necessary it may appear, resistance always also amounts to an intractable tautology. It just resists. As it resists something, this or that, there is an excess in resistance without which it would turn into a force of normalisation and normativity, integration and institutionalisation, consensus and conformism.'—Letter from Alexander Garcia Düttman to Juan Manuel Garrido, 2015. Available at: https://bit.ly/2xYy6PR (last accessed on 21 September 2020).

being done—sometimes in risky activism, or even agitation, but often in discreet, patient, stubborn fervour.)

It is in process precisely because it has never happened that a heap of confusions has not also produced perceptions (as Althusser says) and demands that measure up to them. It's a question, actually, of realizing to what point something is done: what profound transformation is underway, what decisive metamorphosis of the history of the world or worlds (cosmic, poietic, praxic, theoretic, spiritual pluriverses).

Or rather, not even 'what' transformation—since it is merely underway and will only be a little intelligible in, at best, two or three centuries. But at least *that there is a transformation*. That is far from being a first in history. But it is the first that knows itself as such with as much acuity, because it follows a long habit of planned, anticipated history, history that has been aimed at in its realization. So we experience even more strongly the upheavals that thwart our expectations and disturb our habits.

4

Transformation does not mean return, or abandonment, or non-intervention. It involves the unforeseen and the unforeseeable; so it exceeds the already-anticipated possibilities. It certainly exposes us to the impossible—that is, to what defies any identification, any recognition, any assimilation.

It particularly requires opening up worksites on the very places of confusion and powerlessness. On the very place of 'doing' and 'politics,' since that is where we always expect and demand the doing, the effectiveness of the decided-upon action. If our expectations are disappointed, it's not because the political actors are bad: they are what they can be, since they are instantly involved in trompe-l'oeil. We make them act, and they, generally, do nothing but perform. Perform what? What a huge mechanism tends to realize, the production of a whole at once total and infinite, totality in an endless expansion of a circulation of forces and forms, informations and conformations—a production redoubled by an equally interminable multiplication of general equalization of all things and all beings measured by itself, by its inexhaustible convertibility into its own potency.

In the end, capitalism represents the only effective attempt to produce a second world that would be 'entirely the same as the first,' as Descartes said, and yet basically distinct: a world as a replacement of the world, that is, of all possible worlds by a second world bearing in itself its own end. With the sole reservation that this end itself turns out to be endless, or infinite, in the sense of interminable and inexhaustible.

The opening of the infinite in the finite was the decisive transformation of the ancient world. The infinite opened onto two things: onto the interminable, and the absolute. Production, and adoration. Production of goods, appropriation. Adoration of nothing, ecstasy and abandonment. Not without the two aspects touching each other, contaminating each other, getting mixed up in each other to the point of confusion. Internal dissension of the West spreading throughout the world. Confusion is perhaps now at its height and heading towards its decomposition. But we will not rid ourselves of the intersection between finite and infinite: crossroads, gash, wound and suture.

I will not go any further in this metaphysical direction. But let's not lose sight of the fact that, in the last analysis, that is exactly what is at stake. Justice in all its forms—towards starving, oppressed, liquidated, exploited existences as well as towards saturated, overfed, stupefied lives—is not possible without going through a philosophy of the infinite in some way or other. For justice *is* infinite (Derrida calls it 'indeconstructable').

If it is a question of doing, it is obviously doing justice. Any *doing* [faire] has to do with justice. It does justice, undoes it, or counterfeits it. All fundamentalisms, whether they claim a God or a natural law, a supreme commandment or sanctions against competition, necessarily invoke justice. The sensitive spot is precisely here: justice is without foundation. It flows through them and makes them all collapse together.

5

The paradox of Western civilization—that civilization whose civility or culture was as if immediately indissociable from a limitless expansion—consists of the repeated collapse of what it always builds anew. It has emerged from an upheaval of established forms—theocratic empires or local cultures, well-defined regimes of adherence and observance—and for its share has received the task of founding as such, without any foundation available to build on. So it has at once established everything anew and brought to light the infinite aspect of foundation. It made the city (the *polis*) by showing its fragility; it made law by identifying it with its own endless invention; it made a god withdrawn from any sacred identity; (it also converted that god into several wrathful idols, and forged for itself a scapegoat-population of its own defects); it represented the human form (*mimesis*) by showing how much it is without a model; it made up fables of unassignable origins (voids, atoms, emptiness); it calculated the infinitesimal; it enclosed this world by revealing the eternal silence of worlds; it made a general equivalence rule where everything is worth everything, hence nothing; it erected massive sciences around an abyssal non-knowledge. In short, this immense culture, having developed from a philosophy of *creatio ex nihilo*, forged a path for itself towards a *decreatio in nihilum*.

No doubt this civilization has reached a point where it is clearly exposing itself, without any possible way out, to its own paradox. This point is called 'nihilism' and that is what we must leave, in both senses of the word. We must go further, but by leaving from that very point, and not by struggling to cover it up with supposedly 'emergency' structures (humanism, socialism, spiritualism, all the series of -isms of which we are capable).

6

Time is pressing because the task is so lengthy . . . Caught in a movement that has already begun to shift mountains, worlds, forces and forms like that which regularly comes to re-carve and reshape a riverbed, we feel an urgency: an urge to do, and for this doing, an urge towards thinking. Towards weighing the weight of our representations of 'doing' and their insistences. We need time. We need to take the time in the time that is pressing. We need to bathe in the river that is never the same, but, while bathing, we must feel the motion of the flow and the shifting of the shores, the strength of the current. And try to keep in mind the sea into which it finally merges.

On a provisional, exploratory, basis, here are two brief essays—on politics, and on doing. Followed by a text published after 13 November 2015: a symptom of urgency, and of the wish not to rush anything.

'Politics was first the art of preventing people from busying themselves with what is their own business.

'In the following epoch, they added to that the art of forcing people to decide about things of which they understood nothing.

'This second principle combined with the first.'[1]

These words by Valéry date back over a century: to 1910, precisely. We understand them only too well. We also understand that it wasn't even necessary for Europe to begin its own self-destruction in the form of war for politics already to be the object of a cynical sarcasm that has never left it.

Today we say 'political politics' [*politique politicienne*], a strange tautology that further lowers the twofold art Valéry speaks of by reducing his pair to a machination aimed at safeguarding local powers as well as more or less legitimate status and income.

At the same time, we also give to 'politics' infinitely loftier, even sublime, acceptations. The word easily designates, among the most serious and well-regarded authors, the superior region where all of

1 Paul Valéry, *Cahiers, II* (Paris: Gallimard, 1974), p. 1453.

existence takes on meaning. One where the space we share and the space of the singular and the intimate flourish together. The place of full justice or of real happiness. The space of the exchanging and sharing of reason, even of a beyond-space of reasons. Of course there is also the space of higher decision—authority or uprising—that might open (will someday open) that space as such. In sum, the all-power of a life and/or a consciousness developing and accomplishing their being.

If I express it in this way, I seem to be joking. That is not at all the case. I could without further ado gather quotations, but everyone else can do that too. Today a fetishism of politics has spread, one similar to the fetishism of merchandise, and that might correspond in fact to a merchandizing of the thing.[2]

The lofty view of politics—which today means of democracy—is as legitimate and as deeply grounded in reason as contempt of it is justified by continual practices. Lofty goals and rampant corruption argue with each other in discourse as well as in reality. That's why, for example, the distinction has often been made between politics and the political ['*le*' or '*la*' *politique*], or else some have wanted to make a retirement/redefinition of the political along with other operations of continual differentiation and conceptual redistribution over the past 50 years. There's nothing to be done—a seemingly incurable schizophrenia affects the use of the

---

2 Isn't this phenomenon already contemporary with the first politics? Isn't it represented in the Socratic Dialogues? This is what Juan Manuel Garrido has suggested to me (you'll find several mentions of his name in this book, since he helped quite a bit with its editing).

word. It only conveys the fact that the thing itself can no longer know what it is nor what it should and can do.[3]

Or rather it does not know what it should do because the objectives are lacking, and it does not know what it can do because it is constrained by technological and economic powers—by the technology of an economy whose objectives determine everything.

The loss, or at least the relativization, of political autonomy began with the installation of a principle of totality in collective life (unless it's more correct to speak of a collectivization). Two phenomena have reinforced each other: the disappearance of hierarchies, and technological development. They are both inscribed in capitalism, that is to say, in the substitution of the production and sale of goods for the relatively autarkic reproduction of subsistence. The equality of all people in the contest (competition and

---

3 These adventures and misadventures of the word stand out from the background of its ordinary usage which covers three registers: (1) that of social action—itself disconnected from any perspective of the whole, and placed under the sign of certain terms arousing compassion ('inequality,' 'lack of security,' 'exclusion'—to which we want to bring 'care') which only distance even further the realities of the technological and economic transformations (automatization, outsourcing, structural unemployment); (2) that of foreign politics (the more or less usually transparent screen of economic relations); and (3) that of political parties (which either also veil self-interest struggles or are held to confess the profound convergence of their supposed antagonisms or archaistic poverty). It would be excessive to claim that this ordinary kind of politics has nothing at stake: it intervenes in many local situations (on the scale of regions, countries, provinces, cities), and the quality of its actors is not always negligible. But its concept is the regulation of equilibriums—it is not that of a 'meaning,' a 'destination' or a 'configuration' of shared existence.

correlation) of technological initiative and enterprise engenders the exponential development of the sphere we'll call 'political economy'. We can say that the first word tends to absorb or subsume the second. Economy is not just the domination of money (which it in fact permits, especially in all fiduciary, and then 'virtual,' forms): it is also the domination of a complex totality in which technological, market and financial interconnections form an ensemble that depends on its own poles of power.

2

Modernity has created a regime of totality in constant expansion and contraction in which governments have constituted themselves both as regulating poles and actual powers. (Actually, it is no doubt difficult to untangle the antecedences and consequences between the formation of the State and the formation of capitalism.) At the same time, the State represented yet another dimension: as its name indicates (*stato* in Italian, which was its original language), it ensures the stability of the whole which various forces are always on the verge of disassembling.

One could say that stability in more than one respect opposes economic and technological totality which requires innovating market agitation. But it can do this only provided it indicates something other than totality. It would be an exaggeration to say that the State indicates the actual infinite while the economy indicates the potential infinite, endlessly in the process of totalization. But this would not be completely absurd. The modern State with its sovereignty wanted to occupy a place reserved for itself by the supreme being. That is why between State and Church tensions were always as strong as were the conspiracies. That is also why speaking of the 'theological-political' always risks being confused or ambiguous. Either there is divine sovereignty (theocracy), or there is political sovereignty: the two exclude each other, even when they make their shady pacts.

The sovereign State rests on an injustice. It occupies a place to which no mortal has a right. That is also why, as Derrida has shown, the beast can always rise up in the sovereign, fierce and devouring. But it is no less the case that sovereignty keeps or kept open an escape route out of the totality. Exactly the same escape route by which the power to suspend the law by claiming exceptional circumstances is indicated. This authorizes all abuses, but it can also indicate an exorbitant dimension in relation to totality: a basic insufficiency in the economy, or in what with Hegel we can call 'society' as the ensemble of relationships in exteriority, as distinguished from the assumption in 'the Idea in deed' as constituted by the State. Hegel's phrase (in fact 'the ethical Idea', *die sittliche Idee*—which could be conveyed by talking of the 'spirit of the community') is not just his, it also indicates what is at stake: the Idea constitutes the true form, the accomplished reality of the meaning of relations presenting themselves as such, as the unity of a vocation or a destination. What we have long called 'the spirit of a people' has borne the highest aspiration of the politics of the State becoming nation-State, both 'of law' and a transcendent or sacred essence, a form of actual infinity bearing a destination, a meaning.

Politics as the place of the meaning of being together has been the representation or value with which we have continually endowed the Greek, then Roman, city. We thought we made the democratic revolution in that image. Modern democracy, however, stemmed from the principle of totality (connection of productive competition) and not from the principle of shared identity or entity that it wanted to suppose and that it projected onto the ancient cities.

Whether or not this projection has historic value doesn't matter. What matters is that democracy fed the desire to embody in the people the principle of a superior, supreme signification which previously seemed to have taken directly or indirectly divine forms. Athens, then Rome, were sacred in themselves. So they were not really autonomous in the sense that we moderns mean it. With Christianity, the sacred separated itself from territorial unities and peoples. It invented for itself a people of God. The Church modelled itself on the imperial construction, carried to heavenly heights (so much so, we should note in passing, that supposed 'secularization' followed the inverse path of the theologization of a model itself already engaged in a certain form of totalization).

Monotheism bears a philosophy of the Almighty which in principle annihilates any determined Power (by revealing it, precisely, as determined). It thus manifests that it has come from a weakening and devaluing of Powers, whatever they may be (princely, imperial, sacral). Of course, each of the three major Mediterranean versions of this monotheism[4] represents a specific way of dealing with the

---

4 The Zoroastrism that preceded them offered comparable features in opposition to domination (which did not prevent it from being the religion of an empire): we should pause to consider it, just as we should also consider Buddhism, that Eastern contemporary of the philosophical and monotheist transformation in the West.

17

Almighty: but it is possible to understand the Western turning-point as a general shift of Power to an infinite alterity, whence in the same movement politics establishes itself as self-determination and self-limitation of a power unique to the human city *and* desires to equal transcendent power. In the recourse to the superior signification of politics (or of the political), we can often recognize a desire for omnipotence.

3

The desire for democracy barely survives now, thanks to a few symbols sacred to the United States, or in constitutional monarchies. That politics—the institution and existential system of the city—is no longer the condition or place to exercise that meaning of being (of being in the world, of being together and being oneself), we have known for a long time. Heidegger develops this in his lecture on Parmenides from 1942 to 43. His proposal was to assert against Nazism that politics can no longer be the place of the meaning of being (and that, consequently, 'not everything is political').[5]

That philosophers have known this—not all of them, though—did not prevent them from knowing too that economics, technology and society in the Hegelian sense of the word made evermore

5 Of course, we should not forget that at the same time, in his private notebooks, Heidegger regarded himself as a better politician than any of those holding political power, by gesturing towards a hyperbolical politics of the end of the West opening onto a new, destined, radical beginning. (See my *Banality of Heidegger* [Jeff Fort trans.], New York: Fordham University Press, 2017).

fragile the sphere unique to politics: the sphere of a space made up of the public exchange of free deliberation that itself makes sense (I am thinking, of course, of Hannah Arendt).

That is why the withering away of the State was a major motive for the communist movement: a real sense of the common could only re-grow a distinct, autonomous organ within the isonomy of all, instrumentalized in the end by the economy. 'The coldest of all cold monsters,' as Nietzsche said. 'It lies just as coldly, and this lie slithers out of its mouth: "I, the State, am the people."'[6]

It is precisely this lie that Marx, at the outset, wanted to suppress by suppressing the separate position of politics. This had to disappear in order for its true content—what Marx called 'political community'—to impregnate all aspects of common existence. For him, that meant the disappearance of the State, and of 'civil society' which was already the Hegelian name for association in exteriority (of individuals with their needs).

It is remarkable that this was preceded by an entirely different division in Europe when 'civil society' became the recourse against the State or at least apart from it. This occurred with the help of the Polish events starting in 1981. What had a precise meaning in Poland—opposition to a State directed from Moscow—resounded elsewhere with a very different echo. The seduction that was begun to be felt—for example, in France—by the notion of 'civil society' testified to a disbelief in the State of any kind, and preserved traditional criticism through transforming its essential nature. No one

---

6 Friedrich Nietzsche, *Thus Spoke Zarathustra*, Part 2, 'On the New Idol' (author's own translation).—Trans.

noticed that they were simply going along with the progressive erasing of the State under the sway of economic power.[7]

The people, at the same time, continued to become more elusive. Irreducible to the nation, neither a 'great people' nor a 'tiny people', it was reduced (it or its image: the two are indistinguishable) into an electoral clientele, or rather into a population to be ruled. The object of this control was called 'the crowd' or 'the mass', 'the popular masses', precisely when the fall of nation-states was beginning. The population—the people, the populace, everyone— is actually neither a mass nor a crowd without also and above all being the very life of the people, natality in every sense of the word: children, the new, awakening, invention. The people makes and remakes communal existence, innovating and uncertain, adventurous and always exceeding politics as well as any determined sphere—but praxical and mystical, symbolic and real, speaking, singing, suffering, dreaming . . .

4

The State has found itself caught between two declines: one that economic power was headed towards originally, and the one aimed at by the critique of 'political economy'—which is, when it comes down to it, the critique of the modern mode of politics. At the same time, another circumstance had come to reinforce this tendency of

---

7 It was about the model of a civil society detached or removed from the State that in 1985 the *Centre de recherches sur le politique* split and was dissolved, where, along with many others, Philippe Lacoue-Labarthe and myself had been trying to revive the philosophy of politics.

decline. The States that eventually came to be called 'totalitarian' were not States in the classical sense. They stemmed from an entirely different logic: that of the *party*, party in the sense of a formation less destined to seize hold of the State (like factions or rival princes long ago) than to constitute an active body bearing a vital force able to engender a new body and a new existence of the collective. It is well known that totalitarian States, all of them 'socialist' and 'working-class' in their brown or red colours, neglected, or even scorned, the political constitutions of their countries. It is precisely in relation to such a State that 'civil society' stood out in an unprecedented way.

There were two phenomena:

—on the one hand, a long process linked entirely to the technological, economic development of civilization: in this process, the authority and philosophy of the State as 'Idea' of a 'political community' could only pass through the trap of history. This, moreover, explains why the word 'communism' arose at the end of the eighteenth century—as if in counterpoint to Rousseau's 'contract'.[8]

—on the other hand, a twofold reply to this very process, the fascist reply from within already well-developed countries, and the Soviet reply from within a country just about to approach the process.

In both cases, there was a double component: on one hand, the summons to something along the lines of the communal,

8 Cf. my 'Communisme, le mot' in Alain Badiou and Slavoj Žižek (eds), *L'Idée du communisme*, VOL. I (Paris, Lignes, 2010).

community or communism, nation, race, or people, class (in one case a type wanting to impose itself on humanity; in the other, a project for all of humanity); and on the other, the urge to accelerate and intensify the technological-economic and civilizational process.

This twofold reply was given by the power of the process itself, which from without (the North Atlantic and all its partners) and from within (the attraction of the technological-economic dynamism in all socialisms, joined with the weakening of megalomaniac adventures) continually transformed from top to bottom the reality and representation of 'politics'.

We need to retrace the broad outlines of this history to understand that we are at an already advanced stage of a transformation of which 'democracy' and all the images of 'emancipation' are today only weak masks. In this way, we need also to understand that the inflation of the meanings of 'politics' is only the unnoticed effect of the confusion and discredit of the old, classical sense of politics.

Given that we are not going backwards, we must no doubt consider that the model of the State, in any case specified as 'nation-State' and/or as 'State of law', is in the process of being dropped by history back into its old ruts.[9]

The people are now seeking to get out of these ruts.

---

9 This whole business has engendered strong philosophical reflections that have been used to redefine or think anew the very idea of politics. I cannot get involved in examining them, but it would at least be suitable to recall the works of Alain Badiou (his name was already mentioned on the previous page), Jacques Rancière, Étienne Balibar and the Invisible Committee. In various ways, they are all present in the background of this essay.

5

That the State is dated, outdated or expired [*passé, dépassé ou trépassé*] does not prevent the fact that what is haunting us in a stubborn, even obsessive, way under the word 'politics' wants something from us. Economic and technological power can gain as much importance as it wants: it cannot prevent the demands to which it not only does not reply but also that it deceives by its negligence.

These demands are of two kinds. One, that of the minimal significance of the word 'political'; two, that of its maximal significance.

The minimal significance is that of a certain stance: stability, or, the relative balance of powers, interests, needs, the possibility of confrontations, of even clashes in such a way that a being-together can be at least possible, one that does not sink into the panic of generalized violence promised by energies abandoned without any possibility of relationship, whatever the terms of that relationship might be.[10] Looking at it that way, there are politics always and everywhere for human groups, precisely because humanity exists only in groupings. In Heidegger's words, being-with (*Mitsein*) or being-near (*Sein bei . . .*) is strictly co-original in or for being in

---

10 I mean, whether the relationship of human beings is of an emotional, identificatory, symbolic, contractual, fusional kind, or all of those at once, here is not the place to linger over them. Cf. *La Panique politique* with Philippe Lacoue-Labarthe (Paris: Bourgois, 2013).

existence (*Dasein*):[11] that remains the most precise formulation of what was developed as a 'political animal', that is, animal in whom the *logos* requires and permits that being-near or being-with is presented and articulated as such.

This of course comes down to saying also that the group, the assemblage whatever it may be, is a matter of language. It must be named, and, like any signifier, is open both to its own situation and to its own indefinite shifts along the ranges of meaning.

Thus it is necessary for the group to recognize a power. 'Power' [*pouvoir*] is the word our history has placed most in difficulty. We have in practice identified it with pure violence, or scattered it into 'micro-powers'. Between the two, we have managed to lose sight of the transfer of its political exercise into an economic one. But 'power' expresses more than force and something other than rulers, superiors, etc. Power expresses authority, which expresses authorization. In short, legitimization. No political power without a form of law. Pascal's phrase, 'the strong must be just,' is actually always at work, even if it's just to cover up pure violence. For the lie here is worth something like the recognition of a necessity: political animals demand that power symbolize its authority (even at the cost of trickery, which has its limits, as we'll see).

Never in fact has a pure lie covered a pure violence without it finally giving itself away and coming undone. That can take time,

---

11 Cf. also *Being and Time* (*Gesamtausgabe*, VOL. 27 [Frankfurt: Klostermann, 1996]—with thanks to Jordi Masso).

but there is always a mute resistance; yet, as long as that holds true, there is an acceptance of hierarchy—not just in its sense of degrees of command but also in its original meaning: a sacrality of power. It does not need the consecration of a king. It can be content with the consecration of a Constitution and a majority vote.

Hence something of sovereignty functions for any structured gathering of a group: here we're not focusing on sovereignty defined as a particular modality of exercising power; we are designating it as a given inherent in all power. We must recognize the fact that power has the ability to make the final decision. All power authorizes for itself a supremacy, and claims a supreme power that must be recognized as exempt from anything superior to it. This recognition no doubt gestures towards an excess. Excess over any instituted law or excess of a violence that throws off the institutional mask: one can always topple into the other. But that is the condition of all law, even in a religious form. It's only in a sect of madmen that a leader can cause the suicide of the members of his group. Some arch-totalitarian circumstances have brushed with such madness, but only by abandoning all political consistency. On the other hand, the proximity of the beast does not *ipso facto* condemn sovereignty—Derrida himself is well aware of this.

The principle of sovereignty is also inseparable from its opposite: the principle of an insubordination that's just as sovereign. The Universal Declaration of Human Rights of 1948 points out in the preamble that 'it is essential, if man is not to be compelled, as a last resort, to rebellion against tyranny and oppression, that human rights should be protected by the rule of law.'[12] The law affirms here that a 'last resort' can exist to which one can find oneself 'compelled'. If there is a last resort, then the fact of being compelled to it gives it a *sui generis* legitimacy. The force exercised by a sovereign whose work is nothing but oppression loses *ipso facto* its legitimacy, hence its sovereign extra-legitimacy, and changes it into insurrectional extra-legitimacy.

In this way too, the people always go beyond politics—even at the risk of remaining politically out of sight . . .

Any philosophical and theological consideration of any kind of collective structure has always and everywhere borne this reversibility of the principle of sovereignty—often silent, sometimes resounding. Quite simply, if I dare say it, because the very fact of a collective structure implies whatever you like except its destruction. You could say that there is a principle of political identity by which power cannot (this is its basic powerlessness) destroy, dissolve or devour that over which it is exercised. Short of renouncing itself.

Of course, the energy of a force endowed with power tends to exercise it in an unbridled way and to go beyond the service that is its own in order to serve itself . . .[13] But that does not affect the principle of an insurrectional sovereignty.

---

12 Universal Declaration of Human Rights. Available at: https://bit.ly/-3bAzfM8 (last accessed on 21 September 2020).

13 There is an energetic logic of impulse to power and it is not adequate to denounce it. Without it, no one would want to rule, govern or command. Its ambivalence is inherent. That is why one must either control it or reverse it.

The third element of this political minimum can be found in what has traditionally been called 'the art of governing'. An 'art': a technique and a skill, a savoir-faire, calculation and discernment. Plato already speaks of a politics of weaving. Meaning and justice are not given. We must invent them, constantly. We must also constantly justify one sovereignty or other, or rather both together.

6

The maximal signification of politics contains what in whose name the twofold sovereignty functions: namely, communal existence (all people and everyone, neither a 'private' nor a 'collective' existence but one that is shared and sharing, in closeness and in detachment). This existence is recognized as necessary because of the *logos*—meaning, value, of the 'with' or the 'near' that form its very condition. It is recognized as both desirable and dangerous, since the meaning is not given in advance. The 'with' is not a simple, actual given: it is the action of a law that is demanded, summoned, requested. It occurs directly as language, even as the national language (of a people . . .) and speech (of an assembly, a council), and thus as the uttered law [*le droit*]—juris-diction—of Law [*la loi*], juris-prudence—the adjudication of individual cases.

The justi-fication that stands out from the background of this theatre of eloquent tribunal appearance is not given, nor can it be. But its justice imposes itself. It posits this: that the communal must be possible at any cost—except at the cost of itself, except at the cost of communism, of communication or of the community it necessarily already bears without ever being it.

So the implication is that the minimal signification opens onto the maximal: the collective must remain collected because it opens onto the possibility of the communal which is actually its origin and its goal—including the solitude in which each person is born, dies and shares their communal fate. The communal does not exclude the solitary: it implies it as non-totality or as the non-communion of the communal. It is in this way that politics is transcended or exceeded. Infinite origin and goal: that which Christian communion signified in an ambivalent way stemmed from infinity and its constitutive ambiguity. A 'mystical' body—as they said of the body of the resurrected Christ—is a body whose reality evades the indefinite composition of an assemblage and an expansion even though it is present wholly in a multitude of bodies.[14] But this 'wholly' is not a whole and thus is not entire.

That's why it could be not be accomplished in a totality.

Political economy, or one could say economized politics (playing on all possible meanings), obeys only a law of endless totalization. That is why it is possible for it to fail. For it does not escape what minimal politics must contain: the violence of conflict which is just as inherent in the 'with' as the necessity of the communal. Moreover, it is political economy with its naturalistic

---

14 In this way, it is possible to understand how Maurice Blanchot was able to outline a kind of political Christology in *The Unavowable Community*. He touched the depths of the present problem of politics, but with a precisely too-mystical approach not to be called into question. Cf. Maurice Blanchot, *The Unavowable Community* (Pierre Joris trans.) (Barrytown: Station Hill Press, 1988).

fundamentalism—the laws of competition—that aimed at believing in the reduction of conflict in business and communication. It ends up renewing conflict from top to bottom by turning business and communication upside down.

Conflict belongs to language and to meaning because disagreement[15] belongs to them, just as dissensus belongs to consensus. The meaning implies its own rupture.

7

We must be a little more precise on the subject of conflict. The disagreement intrinsic to the possibility of agreement—good or bad— is not limited to the sphere of language. The condition of *speaking animal* implies the possibility of murder and oppression because it implies aspiration to the limitless deployment of mastery that its signification lets us glimpse. Nomination equals domination. And domination wants actual power, power over life and death. This desire is actual and is always renewed by the very desire for meaning—one can even try to say: by this desire that meaning itself *is*.

So we must agree that there is politics—sovereignty and art of governing—first because we must in some way ensure a domination over domination. Probably it is also a matter of allowing the group that dominates itself in this way to accede to some possibility of making the communal, or of making itself communal. But the communal (what 'communism' in principle implies) that actually

---

15 In the sense that Jacques Rancière used it in his book of the same name.

precedes all these conditions and dispositions, which precedes them as *meaning* itself as element of language and of symbol in general (or of relationship), the communal is not simply confused with domination over domination. It is at once more and less. It is both lacking from and in excess of politics: lacking because it indicates nothing—neither sovereignty, nor the art of governing; in excess because it goes beyond this sphere towards other regions or systems where meaning plays in an entirely different way: mastery and non-mastery over life-death (what we call love or art, knowledge or thought).

8

If politics is the art of holding the steering wheel while navigating between two sovereign reefs, this art involves a certain stance and resistance [*tenue et retenue*]. The possibility of an exceptional state of emergency or the possibility of an insurrection cannot be transformed into the more or less acknowledged exercise of domination over meaning itself. That would be the forced suture of what necessarily is ruptured and interrupted [*se rompt et s'interrompt*]. But that does not fail to take place. People argue whether or not there was a 'coup d'état' or a 'revolution' (a just cause of the people). People argue because force does not always let us decipher its nature.

This clash of forces is not avoidable either. Politics cannot be exercised without relating to the meaning of existence. But it can only open *towards* this meaning and *towards* its various modes of being and doing: it cannot even think of subsuming them into one single form. It's not by accident that one of the characteristics of totalitarianism is poverty of thought, art, imagination.

How to resolve the relationship of a political sphere—the one that Marx wanted to see fade away—with the other spheres of existence—in which he wanted to find it diffused? How not to monopolize the meaning while still making possible the maintenance of a whole in which all modes of making-sense are accessible for everyone?

A figure, a fiction might present itself: the Athenian institution of tragedy as spectacle for the city, as financial obligation ('liturgy') for well-off citizens, as a reserve or resource of meaning—sensations, sentiments, sensibilities. It is not by chance that tragedy seems as lost to us as the democracy of that same city. We think it has been replaced by drama given over to sensations and emotions stripped of a sense of existence. But tragedy was situated in a—for us, very strange—gap between the religion from which it had emerged and the politics whose contents it did not convey. No doubt, the oldest wholly preserved tragedy, Aeschylus' *Oresteia*, led to the establishment of democracy. Perhaps, we could say, even in the way Homeric epics contained the models of formation and experience for a society of role models and bravery. The foundation of democracy by Athena, though, as it is played on stage, doesn't occur without a knowing wink when the goddess convinces the Furies to be regarded as the Kindly Ones—without anything having been changed in what had motivated their fury.

Everything occurs as if the very spectacle of politics slightly lifted the curtain from the back of the stage onto a difficult-to-pinpoint, difficult-to-justify strangeness. Everything occurs as if tragedy indicated both the very clear circumscribing of the law *and* its unknown, uncontrollable, vertiginous, worrisome, fascinating beyond.

Tragedy has remained for us the figure of a relationship we may have lost between the city and what in the city exceeds politics: the abysses of meaning (the 'divine'), the enigmas of sensation, the enigmas of emotion, the infinity of truth. That we have (rightly or wrongly) thought we had lost this closeness (or this distance) implies nevertheless that we know something that we find impossible to allocate, control and name: the meaning that exceeds politics as well as politics as irreducible to economy or technology. *And as not destined to give them meaning.*

After the time of tragedy came the time of the first total city—even totalitarian: Rome, which was in itself its own meaning while inventing around it a world, a technological and economic domination, already, of law, urbanism and military order on a grand scale. Sense of citizenship flanked by its investments and diversions. Its model is rooted in our subconscious.

The Church reinforced royal sovereignty by exalting a supernatural sense without in the least preventing the expansion of capitalism. When it was obvious that capitalism was monopolizing meaning (which had been transformed into general equivalence), communism was the speech of a non-merchandized mystical body. But it was not only that: only mystical in the most banal sense of the word, and only indexed onto a value that had to consist of the value of the labour productive of value . . . of a 'human' value whose content remained almost as mysterious as that of 'surplus value'. It was, in the end, the same thing: the value of man producing himself.

In this way, communism, socialisms in general, remained in keeping with a general signification of human autonomy, human mastery of nature and the supernatural, self-destination of the human, and especially of the human in Western culture. The shortcoming of communism was forgetting that 'man infinitely surpasses man' (Pascal) while for Marx 'the root of man is man himself'—by which he explains the notion of radicality and shows its limits.

Autonomy can mean 'not to depend on a law imposed from without'. A slight shift, though, can transform this into 'accomplishing oneself'. But how to accomplish what is never given or discoverable other than as an infinite line of flight?

9

Pascal's saying—which in his letter is quite distinct from a 'poverty of man without God'—resounds like speech that remains yet to be heard.

There is always speech [*parole*]. There is never a last word, never 'true' meaning finally appearing from an illuminated mystery. But for a little while politics has been able to leave access open to something beyond itself. It did not claim to rule in totality, or, rather, it was not compelled to do so. Art, thought, love, faith, fantasy, even knowledge did not bend—or not so uniformly—to the automatism of economic-technological mechanisms.

This automatism has gone as far as it could, reinforcing everywhere the goals of self-: self-management, self-determination, self-production. Politics has conformed to a model of self-constitution [*autoconstitution*] and self-deciding [*autodécision*] that has offered a choice only between an imperious autocracy and a parliamentarism given over to opinion. Today we count votes on one hand, profits on another, both resulting from discreetly manipulated automatisms.

Man, though, is not free, as Spinoza thinks—the only person who thinks out loud what probably all philosophers think more or less categorically. Not free with a self-creating freedom. Freedom is arriving at a heteronomy of meaning: being freed from oneself so as to enter into the intelligence and sensibility of the unknowable, the undeterminable, even the unnamable—but because it is to such an opening that meaning exposes itself. Politics is an administration of possibilities that doesn't impose a higher order on them but opens access to this opening: not what is out of reach, but what reaches us by coming from nowhere and going nowhere. Neither a dream of happiness nor a triumph of mastery, but still and always justice—which is also justice of forms, relationships, emotions, in short, justice of meaning. It is infinitely just that we all can not merely produce a unique meaning but also exist in a circulation of meaning where there is no question of mastering or subjecting.

This can be revealed through art, literature, love, friendship, dreaming or contemplation; but also by the way in which one eats or plays, how we *make do* [*faire avec*] with our bodies, our illnesses, the death of others and our own death . . .

A special example: health and longevity. What are we doing—yes, *doing*—with our medicine? Outside the fact that it is becoming increasingly difficult and complex to administer, it is regulated only via technological possibilities, explorations, treatments multiplied indefinitely up to the borders of death which we try either to postpone or make acceptable. But what if life thus revitalized or appeased doesn't have much to do with existence? It's not so much a question of 'biopolitics'—an unfortunate term when it serves to contrast some unknown 'life' with the grip of power. It is precisely a question of thinking about 'existence' rather than 'life', or rather of thinking about 'life' in an entirely different way. (We should add that Greek *bios* does not mean 'life'—which is *zoe*—but one's mode of existence, social, professional, ethical even. In one sense *bios* is immediately *politikos*. But *bios theoretikos*, for example, exceeds it, like what we can call *bios erotikos* or *bios aisthetikos*.[16] Exceeding, though, does not simply mean being exempt from it . . .)

We should think of life itself beyond 'life' and politics itself beyond 'politics'. Let's call it, soberly, fervour.[17]

---

16 I am not asserting, though, that Foucault made a mistake in Greek by creating this word. Either the mistake goes back to the creation of the word 'biology', or Foucault is well aware, more so than many of his disciples, that it's a question of modes of existence.

17 Elsewhere I've called this 'adoration', a term I won't deny, since it comes from the heart of our history, and it may be the least economic word. But it is open to misinterpretation, and that's why I'm trying out another word here.

10

One more example, to conclude. Faced with the chaotic situation of the whole Mediterranean area, it has often been said that we should never have contributed to demolishing the States that were supporting, at least in a relative way, the armed groups claiming allegiance either to Islam or ethnic and territorial adherences. There are many strong reasons to say this. How can we forget, though, that these States were themselves the creations of a colonial and postcolonial order through which were exercised both the will to dominate and political models already worn out, even hackneyed, in the countries where they were born? To conclude: it is an armed organization, master of a good-sized territory, that seizes hold of the title of 'State' . . . And it makes recruits within our countries whose States themselves, if not puppet governments then at least phantom ones [*sinon fantoches du moins fantomatiques*], are subject to the powers of the global machine. At the same time, by reaction, they are reinvested with 'popular' forces and do not know what to do with them—unless, as always, they play at being the leaders a little under the surveillance of global powers.

What supports the spirit and the leaders we call 'popular' or 'populist' does indeed have to do with a certain people: with the people that finds itself deserted by the fundamental movement that is carrying economy and technology with it (formerly progress and modernity . . .). Abandoned on the one hand to unemployment (technological changes, outsourcing, etc.) and on the other to misunderstanding (there is no longer any credible representation of a future, or hierarchy, or *Sittlichkeit*). This people is made up of both the 'middle class' and the *déclassés*.

Global growth is answered by a global refusal. 'Leftist' politics has continually supported the transfer of power to economy without realizing it. It has trusted a 'progress' that was immediately global—material and spiritual—based on the in-principle limitless growth of a power that cannot be compared to any kind of law, symbol, totem or taboo. 'Political economy' made politics useless, or rather, more subtly, placed it at its own service—making us think that 'emancipation' necessarily came by way of it. Isn't it rather a question of freeing ourselves from this emancipation?

The politics of the far right is caught in the opposite contradiction: it is playing with mystical appearances (symbols, totems and taboos) in order to attempt another way of capturing the power to which it nevertheless yields—or rather, in the end, liquidates itself.

Religion in all this is not just a pretext, although obviously it is also one. It also constitutes a sign. It does not speak of politics. It speaks in a fantastic way of that which exceeds politics. Of that which is 'beyond'. Fantasies, hallucinations, addictions. But why? Because it is the most immediate way out when the global stifles and deadens. It is fervour led astray.

11

Religions are not alone. There are many ways, including philosophical ones, to fantasize and practice addiction and going astray:
words, arrangements of words, concepts are not lacking. It is not
by chance that politics has always been a matter of speech, the art
of oratory, persuasion, discourse and rousing chants. Living in *logos*
involves deliberation and its opposite: the grandiloquence of those
who know they are on the verge of the impossible. In this sense,
religion, philosophy, doctrine, knowledge, thought, are always on
the point of letting themselves be used to simulate the beyond of
politics that politics points to.

But 'beyond' [*par-delà*] does not exactly designate a hereafter
[*au-delà*]. It is not a question of transcendence or second coming.
No revelation or unveiling. *Beyond* is happening in this very place—
among other things as the *people*, even if they are nowhere to be
found. We are already there, or rather we pass by there constantly.
We come and go beyond the here and now, returning there, leaving
there. The ways out are not at the end, in an apotheosis, but here in
discreet palpitations, in movements that have already passed
through. Passed through us. Without our knowing it, but what
matters is less what we know than what, without knowing it, we
do with fervour.

We do. In fact, that belongs to existence. By putting aside the
question 'What to do?' I may be continuing to subject myself to it
and to answer it.[18] It is a question that has become overpowering

---

18 An objection made by Juan Manuel Garrido.

with the vanishing of transcendent destinations. 'Doing', however, is indissociable from 'existing': ex-posing oneself also includes exposing oneself to grasping or inventing goals and tools, relationships, results. We make our life and our death, which in turn make us. People will object[19] that we do not 'make' the death inflicted by illness, even less the one caused by murder, attack, torture, sacrificial punishment or savage exploitation (all of which is sometimes confused in a terrifying mixture that claims to be active, operative, efficient and productive). This is true. But it is also a question of that which acts, agitates, destroys and convulses a collective existence capable of unleashing itself against itself without finding any other way out of the conflict than conflagration. We are thus ex-posed to this violence that belongs to the communal: this does not make it admissible, but it urges us to think of the conflict even more in terms of the intimacy of the communal, how it calls for politics and how it demands more and other than politics (in politics or beyond).

For we make—in a semi-transitive sense, like 'making love', *se faire du souci* [worrying], *faire plaisir* [pleasing], *faire peine* [harming]— hence in a sense where making is always also a *se faire* [making ourselves], a matter of being and not of producing. Since 'making' seems to us most often the production of a result, it is however indissociable, even indistinguishable, from a continuous transformation that always demands remaking or perfecting

---

19 This time the objection comes from Cécile Bourguignon, another companion of this book.

[*à refaire ou à parfaire*] at the same time as it unmakes, unties that result from its final appearance.

We make because we exist. Even so. Our existences are by themselves (even if imperceptibly) disruptions, edges, fissures in global functioning. Through these cracks, these gaps, possibilities for disturbance constantly slip.

For we make, we do, that is certain, and it is less a matter of discovering a new object to produce—even if it's conceived of as 'community' itself, which is in fact the most dangerous thing—than of shifting, transforming, modulating or modalizing [*modaliser*] our doing. 'How to do?' then takes precedence over 'What to do?'[20]

We pass beyond furtively, without making a system or a law of it. It is an emotion, an effort of speech, a gesture, a way of giving up control. But that means that both extremes of politics are there, quite close. Insurrection and/or fervour. It is also *to make a people* [*faire peuple*]—but this making is not productive, or operational, or functional, or solely political. But it makes sense . . .

So-called consumer society is already experiencing a kind of exhaustion. Hence a whole section of global power—of so-called developed nations—is worried about losing its hegemony. Where on the contrary it is growing, though, another history is carrying it, another *sittliche Idee* [ethical idea] that is perhaps neither *sittlich*

---

20 A sign, here, towards 'the coming insurrection' and its 'invisible committee'. By indicating that 'what is coming' does not aim (only) at a future but a present in the process of being made: of *se faire* (doing) as a 'how'.

nor *Idee*, which perhaps differs hugely from what we mean by 'meaning' (or 'morals') and by 'Idea'. Hence it differs too from what we have meant by 'politics' and perhaps even—who knows?—by 'economy'.

Whatever the case, what has since Mediterranean antiquity and throughout European history been called 'civilization' is in the process of leaving its accustomed paths and landmarks. For a long time it has projected itself forward as the production of a glorious future; it is now starting to fling itself backwards.

Every person who falls has wings.

Writes Ingeborg Bachmann.[21]

12

What is at stake, without a doubt, is property—the possession and ownership of whatever and whoever it may be, by consumption or production, by exchange or usage. It is the exponential nature of an appropriation that is beginning to be recognized as fruitless and dangerous simply because there is no proper 'subject' of its captures and confiscations. When Marx declares that the negation of capitalism leads to an 'individual' property—hence neither private nor collective—we must understand that this property is not the possession of goods by a subject (a private or a moral person) but,

---

21 From her poem entitled 'The Game Is Over' (Das Spiel Ist Aus). Available at: https://bit.ly/3aASvrH (last accessed on 21 September 2020).

rather, the formation of an existence of its own, opening up to its proper meaning without alienating it from whatever property there may be (material or moral). The word 'individual', then, designates a reality that Marx doesn't know how to name differently—and we don't know any more than he did, but it could be less ill-named by Heidegger's *Dasein* and hence by the *Mitdasein* that is co-essential with it.[22]

It is existence and the sharing of this existence that can alone lay claim to the 'proper', that is, to meaning. A meaning that is not available or discoverable otherwise than in its passage and its sharing—human lives with their exchange of signifiers. People, peoples, *we* never wholly determined, like the one that Conrad Aiken hears speaking:

> And [we have] felt the nothing that sustains our wings.
> And here have seen the catalogue of things—
> All in the maelstrom of the limbo caught,
> and whirled concentric to the funnel's end,

---

22 Going from Marx to Heidegger raises the question of the 'communal' in 'with' and hence the question of the form of the bond of each 'one' to the ensemble of others (and all beings). It also risks dulling the question if we forget that Marx links 'individual property' to 'cooperation and shared possession of all means of production' (*Das Kapital*, I, VIII, 32). We cannot neglect the communal modalities of 'individual' appropriation: the latter stems no less from what Marx first called 'the individual joy of recognizing my personality as an actual power' (*Manuscripts of 1844*). How to think of a cooperative of individual joy? That would be the scarcely humorous form of the question of a politics capable of surpassing itself . . .

sans number, and sans meaning, and sans purpose;
save that the lack of purpose bears a name
the lack of meaning has a heart-beat, and
the lack of number wears a cloak of stars.[23]

---

23 Conrad Aiken, 'Stage Direction' in *The Coming Forth by Day of Osiris Jones* (New York: Charles Scribner's Sons, 1931), p. 3.

WHAT TO DO?[1]

What to do? This question is posed, it imposes itself, I pose it to myself and I pose it to you because we all pose it to ourselves; in this sense, this 'subject' straightaway prevents us from entirely transforming it into a 'theme' and consequently 'treating' it. There can be no 'treatise' on the question *What to do?* unless one defers replying to it, and one can reply to it provided one not only articulates a response but also *does* something.

We all ask ourselves this question today, in this beginning of the second decade of the twenty-first century, in an era that has many reasons to wonder precisely how much it qualifies as an 'era' and whether it is carried beyond the measure this term implies, thus carried into another era, or beyond the possibility of merely thinking of the beginning of a new era. This possibility has up to now no doubt accompanied the successive arisings of the question *What to do?* It may be that this possibility is now exhausted, or profoundly transformed.

---

1 The first version of this essay was a lecture given at the Société française de philosophie on 17 March 2012 and published that same year in the bulletin of that society (NO. 106.2). The text was reprinted in *Appels de Jacques Derrida*, a collection edited and introduced by Ginette Michaud and Danielle Cohen-Levinas (Paris: Hermann, 2014).

We ask ourselves this question on our own and because others ask it of us. It's even its repeated reappearance that has come to mean more than 'the idea', the feeling of a necessity in the choice of this subject. Invited to speak under the auspices of the Société française de philosophie, I felt it impossible to forget that such a Society is today encountering a kind of reversed image in a philosophy of society; I mean in this remarkable phenomenon that makes the signifier 'philosophy' abound in what we call the *media* or in ordinary culture at the very time when the discipline is suffering elsewhere from the same lack of interest affecting the 'humanities' in general. Philosophy as 'phenomenon of society' represents a hasty, approximate, complacent way of answering the anxiety of a more or less explicit *What to do?* Nothing other than an expectation and a demand that will no longer be satisfied by the propositions of politics or religion—at the very least, by simplifying things, for European societies, but there is more than one sign that invites us to enlarge the statement.

But, after all, isn't that how philosophy began? Pythagorean, Socratic or Cynic, it was first the proposition of a *doing*, of an acting in a world where the given rules were beginning to vanish, along with the assigned roles, the models and purposes of existence. It can be shown that a concern to *do* has always underpinned, if not commanded, every other philosophical concern, of knowing or thinking. At the same time, what determines this concern is directly realizing what *doing* means, and how, consequently, the very meaning of a *doing* can or must be resolved.

2

Undertaking a history of the question would be excessive. In 1994, in a debate at the Sorbonne between Alain Minc and Jacques Derrida organized by the 'Nouveau Monde' association (whose name ['New World'] implies trust in what is being done and in what is still to be done), Derrida could put forth the question: *Que faire—de la question que faire?* ('What to do—with the question What to do?'). The em-dash of suspense obviously served to keep the question (we must ask ourselves what to do, once again, or *anew* he even said), while still signalling its already citational nature, recognized, perhaps well worn, hence to be taken up again, renewed and replayed.

I will not comment on this text: I want rather to note that, almost 20 years later, we are both led back to this question with an increased intensity compared to the urgencies felt by the participants of the 1994 debate—and made even more reserved, even sceptical, towards the very possibilities of calling attention to and engaging a *doing*. Derrida revealed that the question had experienced two remarkable circumstances in modern history: that of Kant, and that of Lenin, each time on the eve of a revolution. We could go so far as to say that modern history can be scanned from the return and shiftings of the question.

For it does shift. Kant's question is not exactly 'What to do?' but 'What should I do?' As a question, and as one of the four questions that reason imposes on itself, it exhibits the modern erasure of a given *duty*, constituted in aid of a duty to be aimed at, planned (under the rule of the universal, as we know); but since this question finds its answer in 'rational common knowledge' as Kant says, it shows the intrinsically *practical* nature of reason. That means that reason acts and is ordered to act by itself, without going astray as it does in its theoretical usage, but without being able to determine (schematize, in Kantian terms) the object of the universal plan of action. The question has an answer in the form of a regulating aim: it's a matter of acting *as if* a universal goal could be found.

In more or less direct ways, the heritage of this 'as if'—which would experience with Vaihinger a particularly notable recasting by its effects on Freud or Kelsen—will have guided all reformative or transformative undertakings regulated on what Nietzsche (hardly expected in this filiation) called 'regulatory fiction'. Admitting the fictive nature (or fictional as we say today, in a kind of prudent litotes) of the sought-for goal implies a dissociation between the *doing* of action and the goal that should be its own.

The first positing of the question *What to do?*, as a question of duty, implies an internal dehiscence of doing: it is commanded *and* its execution is not objectifiable. That is why it is commanded *despite* its possibly unrealizable nature. This dehiscence is that of pure reason itself insofar as it is practical: it commands itself to make a rational world (insofar as it is subject to moral laws). So it commands itself to realize itself, although its final realization can only be 'postulated'. And it's because it is postulated—because it is so and because it is *solely* postulated—that realization must be the object of a command.

We can say that the modern history of the relationship between theory and practice (a history started in Kant, by a well-known text) is divided between maintaining dehiscence and the demand to reduce it. The decision hinges between the fictioning [*le fictionnement*] and the realization—the *Verwirklichung*—of reason (or however you'd like to call it, Idea, Humanity . . .): either we resolve on utopia and whip up the imagination, or we demand an effectiveness, including by armed struggle and seizing power.

3

The question *What to do?* in its simple state, if we can call it that, freed from the reference to duty, implies that the duty is known, the goal determined. The first occurrence[2] of this question is a literary circumstance—a fiction: it is the novel by Nikolai Chernyshevsky published in 1863 under the title *What Is to Be Done?* The huge success of this novel explains why, in 1902, Lenin re-used the title of a book that had made a deep impression on him ('burrowed into' him, he said). A romantic portrayal of a new kind of humanity, libertarian and sensual, Chernyshevsky's novel had first aroused quite violent reactions from Tolstoy and Dostoyevsky; these reactions, however, remained powerless faced with the dominant infatuation with the book. Chernyshevsky's title can be interpreted in two registers: on one hand, what is to be done is the creation of these 'new humans'; on the other, what the artist

----

2 If we exclude the article 'Quoi faire?' by Babeuf published in 1795 in *Babeuf, textes choisis* (Claude Mazauric introd.) (Paris: Les classiques du peuple, 1976).

must do is provide a 'manual for life.'[3] We could say that it's exactly with this novel that the question found a strict point of equilibrium between fictive representation and realization, with each referring to the other in what constituted for Chernyshevsky an extrapolation of Hegelian aesthetics.

When Lenin repeated the question, fiction was no longer at issue—although his text contains an interesting remark: to the 'reveries' of those he castigates, he contrasts the necessity for another kind of dream, the dreams we try to realize and for which we can speak of the 'connection between dreams and life'.[4] But the question has clearly become a question about means. These means are not immediately given without a specific reflection on the goal. When we think about what was being played out from 1902 onward, we understand the importance of this reflection. Where *What to do?* could first seem like a 'how to do?' a testing and a moulding had to emerge progressively, even a transformation of the representation of the goal itself. We have not yet finished today with evaluating to what extent this process entailed an alteration, an alienation or a betrayal of the goal, or else to what extent the goal itself has been represented and aimed at in a way that doomed it to recede ever further into a fiction that had lost every kind of regulating function.

---

3 The expression can be found in Chernyshevsky's thesis on aesthetics, *The Aesthetic Relationship of Art to Reality*, published in 1855. Available at: https://bit.ly/2Vzocxh (last accessed on 21 September 2020).

4 Lenin uses a quotation from Dmitri Pisarev. Available at: https://bit.ly/-2Y3pPox (last accessed on 21 September 2020).

Whatever the case may be—and It is no small caoo —what we
have here to consider is the fact that this historical undertaking
stemmed not just from Marx and from the demand to 'transform
the world' (*verändern*, make it other) but also from a whole climate
of practical or praxical demands to which Chernyshevsky, among
many others, bore witness.[5] It's in this way that philosophy came
to think of itself as having to be realized. It's not just a matter of
Hegel—for whom this 'duty' is confused with the efficacy of history
(although, we should note, it was not without a lack of vitality and
colour when the twilight *grey* of philosophy occurred)—or of Marx,
for whom the production of reason is nothing but the social production of real existence and value, but it would be at stake much
later with Husserl, who in 1936 calls for the *Verwirklichung* (realization) of 'metaphysics or universal philosophy'[6] as what is at stake
in the 'struggles between the philosophies'. 1936 was three years
after Heidegger's *Rektoratsrede* and two years after his resignation
as rector. In his speech, Heidegger declared that 'the self-assertion
of the German University', that is, the self-effectuation of 'science'
which 'is philosophy', comes down to 'understanding theory itself
as the highest *Verwirklichung* of authentic praxis'.[7]

---

5 To limit ourselves to one name, we should not omit pointing out that
Kierkegaard represents in the same era an entirely homologous demand
but at the other end of the philosophical spectrum.

6 Edmund Husserl, *The Crisis of European Sciences and Transcendental
Phenomenology* (David Carr trans. and introd.) (Evanston, IL: North-
western University Press, 1970), p. 15.

7 '[T]heory was to be understood as itself the highest realization of
genuine practice.'—Martin Heidegger, Karsten Harries and Hermann

On either side is the same desire for effectuation and the same struggle for effectuation, but on the one hand in exclusive trust in theoretical means, on the other a readiness to entrust concern for victory to the most brutal force. The contrast is not balanced; far from it. On either side, still, the motif can be spotted—which neither one would have wanted to call 'regulating'—of an assumed unity of theory and practice: thus, of a reduction of dehiscence.

4

The more or less clear desire to surmount dehiscence and somehow to assert the truth in action—in *entelechy*, says Husserl—of practical reason, or whatever name it's given (an authentic existence, a *'praxis totalitaire* [totalitarian]' as Sartre wrote, meaning 'totalizing'[8]—this desire came undone around 1968. No doubt it's even possible to say that 1968's most profound influence, on the level of thought, was a tension passing to the limit of this desire, surpassing the aim of a theoretical goal by a practice regulated by it, hence surpassing the registers of strategy, politics, and ending up at a singular *praxis*: that of an intransigent *hic et nunc* [here and now]).

Heidegger, 'The Self-Assertion of the German University: Address, Delivered on the Solemn Assumption of the Rectorate of the University Freiburg the Rectorate 1933/34: Facts and Thoughts', *The Review of Metaphysics* 38(3) (1985): 467–502; here, p. 473. Available at www.jstor.org/stable/20128182 (last accessed 13 May 2020). [Translation modified to be more in keeping with Nancy's French version, which uses the term Verwirklichung for 'realization'.—Trans.]

8 Jean-Paul Sartre, *Critique de la raison dialectique* (Paris: Gallimard, 1960), p. 754.

The consequence of this was twofold: on the one hand, the rejection of transformative, even revolutionary action; on the other, the assertion of the immediate effectiveness of a revolution as already accomplished. That's what phrases like '*Vivre sans temps mort et jouir sans entraves*' (Live without any time-outs and enjoy freely') or '*Faites l'amour, pas la guerre!*' (Make love, not war) meant. I'll permit myself a brief personal memory: that of sharing with a para-Situationist group the proud refusal to take part in the creation of a 'Critical University', a project we thought remained prisoner to the idea of 'project', precisely, allied with that of the 'institution'.

Critique of the 'project' as submission to a finality had been Bataille's, and it had been expressed scarcely 10 years earlier, for example, in these terms: 'For me there's an impossibility of agreeing with the principle on which real action in an organized society rests. [. . .] Unconditional refusal is the assertion of my sovereignty.'[9] And this: 'We are entering a world where acquired knowledge will generally change man into means. [. . .] We must define what is not reducible to this transformation.'[10]

Everything occurs here as if, on the one hand, it had become imperative and imperious to *define* what Kant had posited as the *dignity* of a precisely undefinable *end* (man), and, on the other, no less imperative and imperious to posit, thus not only a notion projected

---

9 Letter to Dionys Mascolo, 22 June 1958, in Georges Bataille, *Choix de lettres 1917–1962* (Paris: Gallimard, 1992), p. 482.

10 Letter of 12 July 1958 in Bataille, *Choix de lettres*, p. 490.

in a more or less regulating way but also an actual, unconditional assertion of what is called 'sovereignty'. Without removing ourselves from a task *to do* that can be recognized under the name of 'communism'. Bataille introduces another dehiscence, which we could say is the opposite of the previous saying: no longer a split between theoretical goal and practical possibility but between an already given, irreducible effectiveness and a pragmatic progression that must extend the possibilities of its affirmation.

'68 and Bataille show two symptoms—quite distinct—of a movement of torsion that occurred (on a global scale) in the period when, for the first time since 1945, revolutionary perspectives were being transformed, along with the awareness of history and its various progresses, technological innovations and geopolitical balances. Ernesto 'Che' Guevara died in 1967, the originator of the phrase 'Be realistic, demand the impossible.'

If up to that point *What to do?* had been connected either with the aim of an ultimate goal, or with the discovering of judicious means, it is now the *doing* itself that is undergoing a modulation just as characteristic no doubt as the one that made it emerge into the broad daylight of history and thought. The matter of *doing* is not playing out solely on the register of the project nor of militancy (the question has precisely arisen in the meantime from the sense of militant action that sacrifices its actors). It is no longer being played out from the point of view of at least potentially adapting means to ends. On the contrary, we must recognize in *doing* an unusual kind of distinction. The dehiscence between theory and practice, and then the will to reduce the gap in carrying out the project, are followed by a questioning of *doing* itself.

It would without a doubt be possible to show how this history has been especially illustrated in a succession of repeats, glosses and interpretations of Marx's eleventh thesis on Feuerbach, which states: 'Philosophers have hitherto only *interpreted* the world in various ways; the point is to *change* it.'[11] The extraordinary destiny of this thesis shows how keenly it touched the nerve of an era: the feeling of an urgent need to do. I will not attempt to retrace this abundant history. I'll merely point out that Derrida, in a lecture that will be discussed later in this essay, still felt the need—if I can put it that way—to go back to the famous eleventh thesis and emphasize, among other things, the word *verändern*, which does not mean quite the same thing as 'change'.

In fact, *verändern* means 'make other' or 'alter'. When one translates this as 'change', its relationship to 'interpret' ('only interpreted') seems like a relationship to *Verwirklichung* (realization): (theoretical) interpretation provided the formal condition for a change to be made. This would be Hegel reinstated, or *Geist* (*esprit*) understood—and understandable—as self-production of social, human, even natural existence. However Marx understood himself, *making other* suggests a different meaning: whereas interpretation leaves what it interprets intact, like a text whose literality is preserved, even in opacity, *Veränderung* would write another text.

---

11 See Marx, *Theses On Feuerbach*. Available at: https://bit.ly/2Kxga1t (last accessed on 21 September 2020).

This text would be less the realization of interpretation than the invention and putting into play of another world, that is, another configuration of meaning. Nothing would be identifiable any more with its literalness intact.

The result of this is that the implied *doing* is not the same: in the first interpretation, it is a production, a *poiesis* conceived as starting from the rules of art (for instance, the action of the proletariat as realization of the fecundity of the negative); in the second interpretation, it is an *acting*, a gesture that on its own holds its form as much as its force. It is not applied to the world; rather, it makes the world in the way that the gesture—the touch, hand and palette [*la patte et la palette*]—of a painter make the world that is his own. But then it is a *praxis* that is at stake, and the production, the work [*oeuvre*] are important only as they manifest this *praxis*, that is this in-transitive *doing* which by doing makes itself rather than something else.

5

It is perhaps around the meaning and issue of *doing* as *praxis*, or *praxis* re-actualized by Marxism in a certain indecisiveness of its meaning in relation to its Aristotelian usage, that the meaning of the question *What to do?* has most profoundly been played out—to the point of making the question *What to do with this question?* apt.

In her chapter entitled 'The *Vita Activa* and the Modern Age', Hannah Arendt describes how the relationship between theory and practice has been turned upside down (one can translate thus the word *Umstülpung* that she uses)¹⁷ insofar as the practical finality in (and not 'of') the *theoria* understood as contemplation has given way to the meaning of *do* as production, in its turn determining 'theoretical' thought as productive force and consequently operatory rather than contemplative. Truth as something *verifiable* shows this: it is truth *made*, produced. *Doing* itself is modified from the value of 'acting' or 'exercising' (as one exercises a profession) to the value of 'producing', 'realizing', 'executing'. Arendt says that *Tun*—whose semantic amplitude is not far from that of 'doing'—detaches itself ever further from *Handeln*—which designates the acting of conduct, relationship.

Without lingering here over Arendt's treatment of this question, we cannot avoid considering the ambiguity introduced into *doing* when it is understood as both transitive and intransitive, or, on the contrary, the simplistic unequivocal quality created by the complete absorption of the intransitive into the transitive.

This absorption had a name: 'action theory' [*actionnisme*], which originated in the artistic realm but was sometimes extended to the political sphere in the German-speaking context. The word 'activism' constituted a rather remarkable Anglophone echo, since it was used more frequently. The activist is confused with the militant, and even often with the leftist (or 'radical') militant. In 1969,

---

12 Hannah Arendt. *The Human Condition* (Chicago: University of Chicago Press, 1958), p. 314. The French translator translated this word as *renversement*, in keeping with the first version of the text, 'reversal' in English. The English version spoke of 'contemplation and action' while in the German version written later on this is 'Theorie und Praxis'.

Adorno published a text[13] that was very critical towards what he saw as '68 action theory (the reverse, in short, of what I mentioned earlier—but '68 had many different aspects).

Against those who at that time advocated a 'primacy of praxis', Adorno formulates a critique that could seem inspired by Arendt: 'A pseudo-activity is required from a point of view that is that of technological productive forces which at the same time we seem to condemn.' A little further on he goes so far as to write, while quoting with bitter irony MacLuhan's saying 'The medium is the message,' that 'The substitution of means for ends will go so far as to take the place of the qualities of man himself.'[14] What is lacking in this submission to the productivist model is, on the one hand, the sense of the fair balance of questions—'people resort to the automatic blockage of the question What to do?, answering every critical thought before it has even been properly formulated'. On the other hand, no less notably, it is also the sense of the heterogeneity between theory and practice. Adorno declares: 'The dogma of the unity of theory and praxis, unlike the doctrine it claims to be, is non-dialectical: it insinuates a simple sameness where contradiction alone has a chance to be fruitful.'

The contradiction (*Widerspruch*) in question cannot be played out between the meanings of theory and practice: then it would be

---

13 'Marginalien zu Theorie und Praxis' in Theodor W. Adorno, *Kulturkritik und Gesellschaft II. Eingriffe, Stichworte, Anhang* (Frankfurt: Suhrkamp, 2003), pp. 758–82.

14 Using the term *Eigenschaften*, Adorno cannot fail to evoke the novel by Musil (*The Man Without Qualities*).

contradiction in theory itself. It is contradiction between the natures and ranges of two registers, and it implies each one acts on the other to prevent it, in the end, from being what it is, a glimpse of the agitated or impatient mind.[15]

A few years later, in 1974, the syllabus for the French teacher's examination in philosophy proposed (probably not by chance) the question 'theory and practice'. European Marxism, especially in Italy in the Gramsci vein and in France under the influence of Althusser, found itself occupied with open questions in a world that was ever-more distant from the possibility of proceeding to revolutionary action, even though the effectiveness of a number of social, technological and economic transformations was being asserted that theories seemed to struggle to catch up to rather than anticipating.

Here again, the history of this period of profound reshaping of aims, conditions and awareness of *What to do?* would be a considerable task. I will content myself with one sign, again taken from Derrida, who was called on to give a seminar on this subject.[16] I'll point out a motif that in one respect forms its dominant tone, a motif given right away by the commonly used expression '*faut le*

---

15 In the same text, Adorno attacks 'the impatience that wants to transform the world without interpreting it, whereas it has been said in this very place that philosophers have done nothing till now but interpret . . .'

16 This seminar will be published by Galilée (in the meantime, it is impossible to give page references). His text was verified by Alexandre Garcia-Düttmann, who was eager to communicate it to me, and to whom I also owe the text by Adorno quoted earlier as well as the phrase by Foucault cited later on.

faire' [must do it]. (It should be noted that, in 1974, the idiom of the time was still unaware of the current implication '*ça va*—or *ça va pas*—*le faire*' [it's OK—or not—to do it], which is not without some similarity.) *Faut le faire* has the more familiar synonyms—I quote Derrida—'*faut se le taper, se le coltiner*' [must go along with it, put up with it]. The contrast, if not the contradiction, of the practice must stand out in an obvious way, in its difficulty, its harshness. We enter the order of the resistance of materials which themselves are material, human, institutional, etc. The specific weight of *faut le faire* bears this consequence: 'No practice is ever purely faithful to its principle.' This infidelity, also called inadequacy, would turn out to be 'radical and *a priori* necessary' as soon as the practical initiative, the decision to act, can only be what it is provided it is not the pure execution of a program. Or better: a programme cannot programme such a decision.

Derrida would use this motif again elsewhere several times, for example when he wrote: 'No politics has ever been adequate to its concept.'[17] Or, on the subject of the 'practical operation' that is 'sovereignty' according to Bataille, he quotes Bataille: 'Between the time of effort and the sovereign time there is inevitably a break [*coupure*], one could even say an abyss [*abîme*].'[18]

---

17 Jacques Derrida, *The Politics of Friendship* (George Collins trans.) (New York: Verso, 1997), p. 114.

18 Jacques Derrida, *Writing and Difference* (Alan Bass trans.) (Chicago: University of Chicago Press, 1978), p. 336.

6

In any case—and all these cases are very diverse—the initial dehiscence between theory and practice was transformed into a very strong unevenness [*dénivellation*], or was exacerbated into discrepancy, distortion, or a tendential recasting of the two notions.

Thus in the meantime, through these transformations or along with them, something occurred to *doing* itself and in general. The scheme of shifting gears from the theoretical to the practical was used or seized at the same time that the 'images of the world' (the *Weltbilder* of which Heidegger speaks) bestowed on the word 'ideology' a novel meaning, to make it mean a 'logic of the idea' and thus also its *Verwirklichung*.[19] By speaking of an 'end of ideologies', one made more remote the possibility of a will in the Kantian sense, that is, a capacity to make a representation effective.[20]

Though the question of revolution—its possibility, its desirability, its reality—continues to be unsettled, it has on the contrary seemed possible to speak of an 'end of history' that would suspend all recourse to a project, if so many practices calling for either art, or organizational, religious or humanitarian action are offered at

19 See Hannah Arendt, *The Origins of Totalitarianism* (New York: Harcourt, 1976), especially the last chapter, 'Ideology and Terror: A Novel Form of Government'.

20 Cf. an especially clear use of this motif: 'die Kausalität des Verstandes, die Gegenstände seiner Vorstellungen wirklich zu machen,' [The causality of the understanding to make actual the circumstances of its conceptions'—Trans.] *Vorlesungen über die philosophische Religionslehre* (Leipzig, 1817), p. 118.—On 'ideology,' see in Appendix a special 'Note'.

the margins or in place of political action. If *making Europe* or *making peace* are expressions not very distinct from *making believe* to say nothing of *doing your studies* or *doing sports*, it is because the *doing* itself has been weakened.

It has been weakened—made weak and dubious—in inverse proportion to the trust placed in the motif and motive of *Verwirklichung*. Not just that the realization of projects, programmes or plans was no longer credible but also that effectiveness itself was found to be destabilized, or at least its representation. Everything happens as if we needed extremes of suffering or revolt for us to develop a thick skin, material compactness. For the rest, it usually seems to us difficult to untangle the image from the thing, to situate the virtual (a word that has been given an excessive range), just as fiction is turning out to be indissociable from presentation, just as spectacle is slipping into critique of the spectacle, just as the 'impossible' is becoming the other name for the 'real' and just as Melville's story of Bartleby the Scrivener who preferred to withdraw from the *busy-ness* [*affairement*] of the world of Wall Street is becoming a kind of philosopheme [*philosophème*].[21]

If I speak of sensibility, it is not to linger in a psycho-sociological register that would prevent me from either political or philosophical engagement. It is because sensibility acts; it mobilizes thought, it is even its mobility, its motivating spirit [*élan*], its impulse. A will does not want anything unless an *impetus* urges it on. Seneca said so,

---

21 Cf. Gisèle Berkman, *L'Effet Bartleby* (Paris: Hermann, 2011).

along with Ovid,²² and Adorno, in the text already cited, speaks of the 'practical impulse' that urges thought on without it realizing it.

Like a mockery of the question *What to do?* and like a witness to its disinheritance, in 1965 (already), in the middle of the story about the colourful suicide, *Pierrot le fou,* Jean-Luc Godard put these words in the mouth of Pierrot's girlfriend: 'What can I do? I dunno what to do' ['*Qu'est-ce que j'peux faire? J'sais pas quoi faire*'] soon after the word *faire* appeared in close-up on a notebook page.

Not knowing what to do, not even knowing what one could do except 'to prefer not to', is waiting for or questioning the very possibility of a *doing,* about which one still has some notion but whose effectiveness has been lost. In the phrases that Anna Karina (the actress in *Pierrot le fou*) utters while walking along a gloomy shoreline, the effectiveness of the missing *doing* is not that of getting a project underway, nor is it that of a conduct or an exercise. It is neither *poiesis* nor *praxis* in an Aristotelian or Marxist sense. Not knowing what to do comes down to not knowing that one exists, unless it's in a diminished way. *Doing* takes on the value that it used to have in the expression *faire la vie* [to make a living] often equivalent to *faire la fête* [throw a party] and that also stands out in *faire l'amour* [to make love], like in some respects at least *faire la guerre* [make war] or in other expressions like *faire jeune* [to look young] or the impersonal mode *il fait beau* [it's nice out] where this verb takes on a value that seems suspended between being and seeming.

----

22 Seneca, *De Clementia,* II, 2, cites the famous *Et quod nunc ratio est impetus ante fuit* from Ovid's *Remedia amoris,* line 10: 'And what was passion before is now reason.'

62

7

As a reply to the duty-to be [*devoir-être*] or to being as duty and project, *doing* remains yet *to* be done, and keeps with it, along with its *affair* and its *fact* [*fait*], all the distance of that *to* (one is even tempted to say: of *its* 'to'. This distance is negligible as long as a horizon of certainty presents itself on which the actual form reveals itself (the Idea) of the fait accompli, the entelechy. Since the duty and/or the project—one *hence* the other, and vice versa—came to the forefront, we have wavered between regulating dehiscence and revolutionary effectuation. It is remarkable that 'revolution' came to mean as much real action, effective because efficient, as the reversal or turning upside-down of the situation. Revolution has been a regulation realized, and regulation has become a postponed or warded-off revolution.

In this process, effectiveness has been found to be marked with the sign of violence. In many ways, for which Nietzsche, Weber, Sorel, Benjamin and Bataille could be notable witnesses—as well as commentators on Benjamin or Bataille who are closer to us, like Derrida—violence has become the *experimentum crucis* (the crucial experiment) of *What to do?* Violence either makes itself understood as a necessary moment in the effectuation of the Idea—but then it becomes an aspect of regulation—or imposes itself as the sudden appearance of Idea itself in all its omnipotence—but such an appearance bears a name, that of sacrifice,[23] and that is precisely what has vanished from our culture. When there is meaning in

23 Sacrifice is from Latin *sacrificium*, to make *sacer*, make sacred.—Trans.

making sacred—or in making, creating the sacred—one does not ask *What to do?* The operation of *veri-fying* (véri-fier) comes through that of *sacrificing*: it contradicts it, substitutes itself for it or annuls it. The instant effectuation of the project verifies its validity by the intended performance (here and now, making the ideal reign), the *doing* thus put into play attacks the project itself, desacralizes it. Should we feel nostalgia for the world of sacrifice?[24] Certainly not. It was certainly the world of an oppressive anxiety against which the great transformations of the Mediterranean and India from the eighth to the fifth centuries BCE occurred. One could characterize these transformations as two ways of relaxing anxiety: one turned towards an active and productive doing, the other towards an acting of letting go and restraint.

When accomplishment turns out to be desperately interminable, or when the fait accompli turns out to be destruction of its own Idea, the *doing* that was to be done discredits itself or deposes itself. In one sense, the whole history of *What to do?* has not stopped replaying the alternation of its own disavowals. And yet the same history will have emphasized and brought out even more the quality of effectiveness that is the most inherent mark of *doing*.

For this reason, the demand for an effectiveness that is neither project-aimed nor tyrannical has appeared in contemporary thought. If the pattern of history has shifted, forcing us to question the paradigms of revolution and progress and thereby opening the way to patterns of spacing and/or event, it is especially for this

---

24 Question posed by Cécile Bourguignon.

reason. What Heidegger calls *Faktizität* and we could translate as 'factuality' (if this term didn't also have something of the dull platitude about it)[25] designates, at heart, the existential effectiveness of what Kant foretold with the *factum rationis*: less a duty to be carried out than an *exposition* always already given to real, mundane, material exteriority. Less the realm of a practice of a specific and distinct order (moral, political, pragmatic) than the very identity of so-called reason, its rationality in action, its *ethos*[26] as ordinary conduct as well as site or abode.

Doing thus implies this value that opens its semantic amplitude onto either side of production and execution: the sense of *facio*[27] as 'put, place, establish' but 'in a creative way, establish in existence and not simply leave an object on the ground'. What is at stake is doing rather than having to be. These two dispositions, these two tensions have no doubt always divided philosophical ethos—and pathos. But it is remarkable that the most recent thought has, so to speak, felt the need to appear in concurring modes of doing rather than in being, on one hand, and on having to do on the other.[28]

---

25 In English discussions of Heidegger, *Faktizität* is usually translated as 'facticity'.—Trans.

26 *Ethos*, abode, habitat, or *ethos*, conduct, *habitus*, twofold possibility in the background of the motif of 'morals' and of '*Sittlichkeit*' in general.

27 Cf. Émile Benveniste, *Dictionary of Indo-European Concepts and Society* (Elizabeth Palmer trans.) (Chicago: Hau Books, 2016), p. 387.

28 Claude Simon testifies to this sensibility when he declares that his existence is best justified by 'doing': 'It is not Descartes' "Cogito ergo sum" but, rather, "I *do* (I *produce*), hence I *am*", a basic need, it seems to me, and one felt by every normal human who responds to it in one way or another,

8

I will just give a few hints towards an analysis that might deserve the work of a thesis. By distorting the linguistic usage of the word 'pragmatic', I will say that, in the middle of the twentieth century, there developed a kind of philosophical pragmatics that came to be substituted for the theory of concepts waiting to be applied and/or the theory of experimental verification.

This pragmatics is never absent from philosophy. It is even to be heard in Platonic dialogues, in Cartesian and Malebranche-ist meditation, in Spinoza's *mos geometricum* or in the speculative economy of Hegelian discourse, just as it lays claim to itself as such in Nietzsche's aphorisms or in Kierkegaard's 'crumbs'. Each philosophy is a behaviour, a conduct, an exercise of thought—consequently of language in its vocabulary, syntax, rhetoric, tonality.

Thus the work of Michel Foucault has progressively and tendentially been identified not just with actions of sociopolitical reach but especially with a paraenesis of what we'd like to borrow from Montaigne as the word 'exercitation'—to be of 'the mind' is only more perceptibly the state and appearance of the 'body'.

Emmanuel Levinas added ethics to ontology by putting into play a speech that exceeds its own discourse by becoming the 'contact' with an 'original language, the foundation of the other'.[29]

------

whether by *reaping* the crops [en *faisant* venir une récolte], *doing* business, *making* or building a bridge or machines, *doing* research, etc.' (*Quatre conférences*, Paris: Minuit, 2012, p. 76.)

29 Emmanual Levinas, 'Langage et proximité' in *En découvrant l'existence avec Husserl et Heidegger* (Paris: Vrin, 2006), p. 314. In English, see

Deleuze, paradoxically, designates as 'creation of concepts' what is also given as mobilization of words and images according to a kind of permanent performativity: 'rhizome', 'crystal' or 'becoming imperceptible' are obviously more than ciphers of signification; they are indicators of activity, affectivity or effectivity.

By suggesting *différance* as 'neither a word nor a concept', Derrida was suggesting *a gesture*: on the other side of the procrastination that some thought they understood, tension in action—in language and in the body of thought—of a presence in its distance from self.

Two facts can be added to these indeed very different characteristics of a pragmatics impossible to subsume under one identity: one, the importance granted by all these philosophies to literature and art,[30] that is, to an ensemble of spheres where the division between being (or thinking) and doing is straightaway annulled; two, the distance taken with respect to political power. Neither the government of the wise, nor the enlightened council of princes, nor theoretical argumentation opening the way to action are appropriate any longer for these philosophies. This is also because they were able to take charge of a considerable shift in the very idea of

'Language and Proximity' in *Collected Philosophical Papers* (Alphonso Lingis trans.) (Dordrecht: Martinus Nijhoff Publishers, 1987), p. 116. Levinas also expressly calls for a surpassing of the separation between theory and practice, especially in the preface to *Totality and Infinity*.

30 This is true, despite appearances and *mutatis mutandis*, for Levinas. Cf. *Le souci de l'art chez Emmanuel Levinas*, a gathering of essays by several hands, edited by Danielle Cohen-Levinas (Paris: Manucius, 2010). On the other hand, it would require us to speak here, of course, of Adorno, Benjamin, Bataille and Granel.

'politics'. A phrase by Foucault could speak here for them all: 'It is not for philosophy to tell power what to do, but it has to exist as truth-telling [*dire-vrai*] in a certain relation to political action.'[31]

The question *What to do?* does not disappear, but it clearly refers to other spheres whose deviation [*dénivellation*], even divergence, from the philosophical register, are indispensable to measure. Deviation or divergence due as much to the impossibility of *Verwirklichung* as to the excess of a violent *Auswirkung*.

'Truth-telling', for its part, is not a telling-the-truth as a production of verifiable meanings. Rather, it is the praxis of a saying that does not let itself be subjected to any project, which tends only to its own saying and thus to the opening of a sense that is unprecedented every time. This extraordinary nature stems from the incommensurability of an outside with any effective grasp of meaning. It does not call for a *Verwirklichung* but for the actual, present *Wirklichkeit* of an attentive listening, sensitive to the inaudible that is being expressed.

It is not suitable simply to remain silent about what we cannot say: we must understand that 'remaining silent' [*se taire*] is another way of speaking and opening the possibilities of meaning. This moreover is probably how Wittgenstein understood himself. The chances of today are more than ever those of the unprecedented. More than ever Athena's owl is flying off into the twilight. A world is in the process of coming to an end; that is what the phenomenon

---

31 Michel Foucault, *The Government of Self and Others* (Graham Burchell trans.) (New York: Picador, 2010), p. 286.

called 'globalization' means philosophically. We are like the old Stoics of the fifth century who could sense nothing beyond what they called the *inclinatio* of Rome, a becoming that was being set in motion.

9

Like the Romans, we cannot foretell the nature or direction of a transformation whose tremors we can't help feeling, sometime even as jolts, often as convulsions. To tell the truth, our history seems more and more to have erased the possibilities it had at first opened to the question *What to do?* By making 'have to do' into a questioning, it freed it from a given order of goals; by inventing goals ordered by an integral humanity, it designated the horizon of a final production. This horizon was changed in view of destruction and self-destruction: there is no longer for us one single finality that doesn't also bear its hidden side of damage, even disaster, or of indefinite proliferation of new goals. Accomplishments are excesses, entelechies resemble entropies.

No doubt we have made 'doing' go astray by assuming it was the carrying out of a project by putting will into play. This presupposition, contemporary with the entirely 'Practical Philosophy' invented by Descartes,[32] is one whose failure (or at least insufficiency) is recognized by the avowal of a deficiency in philosophy on the subject of action. This is the avowal Heidegger indirectly

---

32 René Descartes, *Discourse on the Method* (John Veitch trans.) (Chicago: Open Court Publishing Co., 1910), Part 6, p. 66.

makes after the defeat that sanctioned his past engagement;[33] it's even the confession that Sartre repeated two or three years later when he noted that action was still waiting for its philosophy,[34] and it's this avowal that later becomes Arendt's lament about the great 'curse of Western history ever since, in the aftermath of the Periclean Age, the men of action and the men of thought parted company and thinking began to emancipate itself altogether from reality, and especially from political factuality and experience.'[35]

How not to acknowledge that we have produced—or, rather, we have produced ourselves—as the subjects of a production that surpasses us as much in how it removes itself from the scheme of its realization as by the fact that it reproduces itself according to the autarchy of a 'doing' given over to its own development. A *savoir (et pouvoir)-faire* [a know-(and can)-do]—that after all is the meaning of 'technique'—is mingled with, and then substituted for, the must-do. But knowing, being able, and having to [*savoir, pouvoir, et devoir*] all leave something of 'doing' intact: precisely that effectiveness which is not that of an object, or that of an active or passive power, or that of the effect of a cause, but that resides in the fact of an existence.

----

33 In the beginning of Heidegger's *Letter on 'Humanism'* (Frank A. Capuzzi trans.). Available at: https://bit.ly/2VEnVt3 (last accessed on 21 September 2020).

34 Jean-Paul Sartre, *Notebooks for an Ethics* (David Pellauer trans.) (Chicago: University of Chicago Press, 1992), p. 50.

35 Hannah Arendt, *On Revolution* (New York and London: Penguin Books, 1990), p. 177.

Such a deed [*pareil fait*] is neither a deed nor is it still to be done [*n'est ni fait, ni à faire*] if I can put it this way by distorting the usage of this phrase.[36] It is doing itself [*se faisant*], in such a way that no subject is its agent, without making itself by doing it. The existent who makes himself relates to himself as to his subject which is not given and does not have to be given, but which is precisely appropriated according to this absence of a given. This absence is in no way a lack: it responds to the essential impossibility of entelechy, that is, to the fact that *telos* is nothing one can accomplish, invest in or realize, for 'reality' is nothing given, nothing produced or producible. The 'doing' that is at stake is done because it is the doing of a 'self', but a self is characterized by the return or infinite return that is not even 'to oneself' since 'self' is already this return of self itself. (A return, I will add, that is thus not to oneself except insofar as it is to the other.)

What to do? as a question implies the aim of a project, an object, an effect. And of course every day we must operate on these registers which are those that must govern prudential (regulating, negotiating, strategic) virtue. But this is not yet 'doing' if doing or acting is letting oneself at the same time be carried to the limits of these registers, where the impossibility of being done with it opens up onto the necessity of *infinir*—if I can risk this term.[37]

---

36 A reference to the well-known French saying *ni fait, ni à faire*, meaning something has been poorly done, botched. Here, *fait* is translated as both fact [*le fait d'une existence*] and deed [*pareil fait*].—Trans.

37 A play on the phrase *en finir* to be done with something, and the word 'infinity'.—Trans.

Letting oneself be carried at the same time to the limits of prudence means exposing oneself to the immeasurability of meaning. Never has meaning been adequate to an object or a project or an effect. It is this inadequacy that is at play. If civilization has entered into mutation, it is because it has begun to understand it by understanding the inanity of its project regulated by effectuation alone.

What to do, then? We must think of *doing* in its deviation [*dénivellation*], in its disengagement even, from the project, the intention and the question. What to do with the *question* in general? Think of the assertion that precedes it, as much behind as in front: the assertion of existing in its exposure to the infinity it is but is precisely not as object or project or effect. Thinking, then, of 'causing to exist' [*faire exister*] without principle or goal, without author or project, but where *existing* is asserted as the adventurous and daring 'shoreless doing' (*uferlosem Tun*) of which Celan speaks.[38] This doing in the poem is that of the mother, whom the text finally names as 'a gleam come from the depths' (*Schimmer aus dem Grund*). A similar gleam, which is also that of the poem, stems from a depth that remains inexhaustible but from which a light lets itself be captured as it comes from this *doing* of the other that does nothing less—or more—than make sense. Making sense as well as making the world, making love, making day and night, making felt,

------

38 Paul Celan, from the poem beginning 'Kein ankerloses Tasten' in *Die Gedichte*, edited with commentary by Barbara Wiedmann (Frankfurt: Suhrkamp, 2003), p. 371. See the chapter titled 'The Mother Figure' in Hugo Bekker's *Paul Celan: Studies in His Early Poetry* (Amsterdam and New York: Editions Rodopi, 1948), pp. 121–2.

all that occurs—Sartre among many others says this—only through and for the other.[39] In the instant of the question *What to do?*, we must not forget that a gleam has gone before, which pointed beyond it.

39 Sartre, *Notebooks*, p. 121.

Note on Ideology

The expression 'end of ideologies' has for a long time functioned as something obvious, one that has been sometimes triumphal, at other times sarcastic and at even other times disillusioned. It has almost been forgotten today (we should remember that it was born in the 1960s, in the title of a book by the American sociologist Daniel Bell: *The End of Ideology: On the Exhaustion of Political Ideas in the Fifties*). There, the word 'ideology' took on the very broad, vague meaning of 'ideological conception that produces meaning'. In 1953, Hannah Arendt had defined it as 'the logic of an idea', namely, the direct deduction of action from an abstract, ideal or imagined concept. In this use of the word resounded the sense that Marx had given it, 'an inverted, illusory representation of reality'.

One could say that the exhaustion of politics in its noble sense (is that word itself ideological? Another question . . .) is in effect the exhaustion of the possibility of representing a sense or a truth of communal existence. But what does 'represent' mean here? Has the sense of Republics, Empires, Kingdoms, Tribes, Peoples that had or seem to have had a lasting consistency been reduced to a

---

1 Added here in 2015.

representation floating in the air like an image painted on a flag, or did it possess the presence and force of that which innervates and nourishes a living body?

You will wonder of what body I am speaking. That in fact is the question: Can we speak of a communal body? And even of a body of the communal? Even metaphorically? (What, for that matter, does a metaphor involve . . . ?) These questions have occupied political reflection since the Classical Age. There is a philosophy and an image of a 'social body' or a 'political body' implicitly subsumed in the words 'community', 'communism', 'commune' or 'council' (*soviet*). There is also for Marx a communal corporeity of nature and man, by which precisely the latter transforms the former and thus produces itself in its humanity. Its human value, neither extorted nor fantasized, is that of the growth of a superior organism where nature and labour are accomplished and surpassed together.

Organicity envelops the power of self-organization, or life. In the new *organization* of the State by the 1789 Revolution, Kant saw an analogy to the organization of nature. Perhaps there is only meaning—of Idea, ideal, model and motive—in a form of life or a living being. It is not a question of 'form of life' in Wittgenstein's sense—that is, of the ensemble of linguistic, representative and practical conducts that allow a communal life. This ensemble is complex, varied and confused; it does not present itself as a coherent ensemble. In one sense, it resembles what used to be called 'the spirit of a people'.

But it is no doubt necessary to consider also what we could call a formative form of forms: the form or Idea that presents itself *as such* and offers itself as transformation of communal life, which is to say, when all is said and done of the communal in which the 'individual' sustains him/herself. Whether or not this form bears the name of a people, a country, an Idea—'communism,' for example, or 'fascism'—it always offers itself as a form of life, of self-organization according to which a being sends, destines or decides itself to itself.

For no one existing, and even no living being, no being at all, stems simply from himself. That would make no sense for what we call inert matter—which, however you look at it, is nothing but interactions, fluxes and complexes—but it makes no more sense for what we call a subject or an *ipse*, a self supposed to keep itself apart, without any possible division.[2] As secret, intimate, inaccessible even to itself as 'oneself' can be (or precisely for this reason . . .), no subject subjectifies or subjects itself, is born, exists or dies outside of the tangle of bodies, desires, native lands, languages, tastes, etc.

This is why self-sufficiency can do nothing here but cause problems, even obstacles. For if a 'form of life' is understood solely insofar as it does not conceive of itself or present itself as a distinct form, a Form conferred on life, on the other hand—more or less by force, inevitably, whatever its legitimacy—implies the certainty and distinction of a 'self' or an 'auto': these in turn imply the ignorance, repression or refusal of the fact that life, in all its forms, destines, decides or desires itself just as well as if it were desiring and destining nothing. Life does not stem from a certainty of self: it is,

---

2 I am using Cécile Bourguignon's terminology here.

moreover, in this way that thought is life itself. The proof is singularly this: that life destines itself to death, desires its death, or desires itself in its death, if we can put it that way.[3]

That does not mean that we are not 'eternal' as Spinoza asserts: the meaning of existence includes life-death, is played through their sequencing and outside it. But that is not the issue of politics—except to immerse itself in 'ideology' or the inverted representation of itself. Politics infused with a fantasy of meaning is mythological politics. Fascisms have illustrated this; theocratism is a more backward form of this today. But whereas myth was the form of the body and life of the peoples it animated, it was neither a concept nor a construct.[4]

Politics is situated between 'forms of life' and the formative Form of a life that would be the immortal life of the 'spirit' [*esprit*]. It must ensure the possibility of an organization that is not an organism, which cannot and must not be an organism. Similarly, it must ensure a constant demand for justice that surpasses it in its actual accomplishment but that requires it in order to be asserted. Similarly, it must allow (but not prescribe) meaningful speech to be invented, which tends not towards myth but towards the *muthos*

---

3 Cf. Jean Manuel Garrido, 'life and death' in *Chances de la pensée* (Paris: Galilée, 2011).

4 I'll permit myself to refer to the first preface to *Le Mythe nazi* by Philippe Lacoue-Labarthe and myself, the fourth edition of which was published by the Nouvelles éditions de l'Aube in 2016, as well as *Proprement dit: Entretien sur le mythe*, with Mathilde Girard (Paris: Lignes, 2015).

heard as speech or, rather, as writing—the trace of what always remains to come for each individual and for each community.

THE WEIGHT OF OUR HISTORY[1]

One would prefer to remain silent. Faced with the horror and the emotion. Faced with the effects of proximity—for what has happened in Paris has not stopped happening for a long time in Bombay, Beirut, Kabul, Baghdad, New York, Madrid, Casablanca, Algiers, Amman, Karachi, London, Tunis, Mosul and so on. Faced with the poverty of our indignation (justified but hollow) or our protests ('we should . . .' 'we just have to . . .')—and the crossfire of points of view (opinion, rebuttal . . .).

One would prefer to remain silent also because of the intense awareness that seizes us as soon as we imagine the inextricable complexity of geneses, causes, chains of events obviously intertwined and enveloped in a global conjunction of great economic and geopolitical clashes. On the level of thought, too, now is not the time for 'we just have to . . .'.

We must, however, try to speak, for the same reasons. Not just because emotion calls for it, but also, and especially, because the

---

1 This text in its first state was written just after the attacks of 13 November 2015 in Paris in response to a request from *L'Humanité*, which published it in *L'Humanité des débats* on 19, 20 and 21 November. It was then enlarged when it was being translated into other languages.

power of this emotion stems from something other than the magnitude of the attacks. Which is nonetheless remarkable—all that coordination, the choice of times and places, say much about the work that went into it beforehand—but there is more: there is the magnitude of a long sequence begun about 25 years ago (to remain within the limits of immediate perception) in Algeria in the 1990s with the creation of the Armed Islamic Group. Twenty-five years, a generation: this is not just a symbolic calculation. It means that a process is unfolding, a maturation is taking place, an experience is being defined. Outlines, tonalities, dispositions have been set in place; nothing fixed or definitive, of course, nothing on which a lid of history labelled 'century' could be fastened; still, a configuration or at least the shape of a turning point, the energy of an inflection, even an impetus.

The force with which the evening of 13 November 2015 in Paris was charged stems from this energy. That is also why it seems immediately to involve a perspective either of a decisive turning point, or of the beginning of a new generation: 25 years in front of us to reach another landing stage, or to pass another threshold. Many of the people shot in this savagery haven't yet had their 25th birthday; they enter this threatening darkness dead or wounded.

The force in question was drawn, essentially, elsewhere than from the resources we call 'fundamentalism' or 'fanaticism'. Indeed, active, vindictive, aggressive fundamentalism—whether Islamic (Sunni or Shiite), Catholic, Protestant, Orthodox, Jewish, Hindu (even at rare times Buddhist)—characterizes the last 25 years in a way that cannot be overlooked. But how can we not notice that it will have responded to what we can designate as the economic fundamentalism inaugurated with the end of the Cold War and the extension of a 'globalization' already underway and indicated almost two generations earlier (MacLuhan's 'global village' dates back to 1967)? How not to point out also the haste to erase totalitarian experiments, as if simple representative democracy accompanied by technological and social progress responded perfectly to the anxieties raised long ago by modern nihilism and to the 'discontent in civilization' of which Freud spoke in 1930?

Liberal fundamentalism asserts the fundamental nature of a so-called natural law of limitless competitive production, equally limitless technological expansion, and especially the tendentially limitless reduction of any other kind of law—political law first and foremost, especially if it means to control natural law according to the particular demands of a country, a people and a form of communal existence. The State so-called of law represents, paradoxically, the both necessary and tendentially lifeless form of a politics deprived of horizon and consistency. Our productivity-oriented, naturalist humanism is itself dissolving and opening the door to inhuman, superhuman, too-human demons . . .

Religious fundamentalism can be limited to the observance of an inflexible doctrine and ritual, with no interaction with the sociopolitical context. When it wants to be active in that context, it presents a twofold demand: on the one hand, it's a matter of rediscovering the force of its mystical foundation; on the other, of allowing this force to cohabit with technological and economic interests so as to enter into their relationships of power. The most

81

eloquent symptom of this undertaking is the adaptation of banking to Islamic law—and vice versa. Another symptom is the war of religions: the Iranian revolution of 1979, while it marked the awakening of a political Islam, also carried to this terrain the major division within Islam. Like those of ancient Europe, the wars of religions respond to social and political clashes. One could say, to simplify things, that the present conflicts in the Middle East—aside from the one connected to Israel—stem from the failure or derailing of the seemingly progressive attempts of postcolonial revolution (Egypt, Syria, Iraq, Algeria).

To a postcolonialization at times hobbled, at times rerouted as much by the interests of ex-colonizers as by relations of force among the ex-colonized, an economic situation has been added that has been turned upside down by increased energy demands and by the transformation of the monetary and financial system. In other words, for two or three generations now, global configuration has engaged in a major transformation of which the conflicts in the Mediterranean and Europe are only one of its aspects—the others occurring in the transformations of the East and Latin America. Fanaticism is finding recruits outside of the world defined too simply as 'Arab-Muslim'.

As for the Mediterranean Muslim world (and here too we are risking a simplification), we must acknowledge that the opposition between Shia and Sunni (which also tallies with the difference between Persian and Arabic culture) is conveyed by a major difference in the way the link between religion and society is configured. The model for a religious inculcation integral to existence, culture and law demanded by Sunni fundamentalism remains in part foreign to the Messianic spirit of Shia (this is said without forgetting the actual behaviour of the Iranian state). That is not without consequences for relations with European and American countries.

These few, oversimplified reminders are made just to evoke the considerable weight of data that lucid reflection must consider. For this weight is precisely the one that makes possible the triggering of fanaticisms as violent and narrow-minded as those we are seeing now. It's when a world is becoming undone that madnesses are exacerbated. It is within mutations that lethal possibilities arise. The Spanish Inquisition or the fanaticisms during the Reformation, like many others (beginning with those of early Christianity and its sects), are no doubt always correlated to critical situations, whether on the social or the existential level.

This weight and this renewed exasperation certainly do not favour the paths to resolution. At least we can, and must, know that we are not faced with the sudden unleashing of a barbarism fallen from who knows what sky. We are faced with a state of history, our history—the history of this 'West' that has become a global machine thrown into a panic by itself.

It would be too easy to condemn this history, just as it would be too easy to seek to justify it. But we must ask ourselves if it is possible to get it out of its own quandary—whether that be nihilist, capitalist, Islamist, or all of those things at once.

Speaking of the capture of Rome by Alaric, Augustine, in Hippo where Roman refugees were flooding in, declared: 'From oppressed flesh the spirit must rise up'. Where can we find the spirit today?

2

Where can we find the spirit today? is a doubly strange question. On the one hand, how can we think we can find 'the spirit', discover it somewhere ...? On the other, the word 'spirit'[2] is one of the most worn-out, even one of the riskiest and most dangerous words there is. It has served both the worst and the best. Still, we cannot forget Marx's saying which described religion as 'the soul of soulless conditions'. In order to designate the absence of something, one must be familiar with that thing. So Marx at least had a notion, a feeling or a clue about the 'spirit'. Marx is well known as a materialist: How can he speak of the soul? He speaks of it because his own materialism is that of the production by man, through his labour, of his own meaning (or his own value as absolute value, not an exchange value or even solely use value).

With or without Marx, one could say that the soul/spirit designates the production of a meaning (as when we speak of the 'spirit of Dante' or 'the spirit of Romanesque art'). Meaning is not a supposedly complete signifier (like 'God' or even 'happiness'); it is a movement by which an existence relates to the world, to others and to itself. This relationship is constantly renewed and never fixed in place (fixed in place, having become dogma or law, it is no longer spirit but inert 'letter').[3]

So it is not a question of finding the spirit, since it is situated nowhere and does not consist of anything able to be situated (like

----

2 *Esprit* can be translated as spirit, soul or mind.—Trans.

3 Presumably a reference to 'For the letter killeth, and the spirit giveth life' (2 Corinthians 3:6).—Trans.

a text or a name or a form, an image, etc.). The spirit is already there in the mere fact of wondering about it, and it is even there when this question turns into anxiety and the feeling of a lack. So it is 'there', in that place which is nowhere but everywhere throughout our actions, our words, our relationships. It is there like the impulse that makes us ask for it.

Too often today we think we can designate it as the spirit of humanism, of law, of what we call 'values'. But it is quite obvious that these words sound all the more hollow the more they are invoked.[4] Spirit is when words are not hollow. When they are, they must be changed.

'Man' [humankind, *l'homme*] is a word that should be changed or recharged with meaning. This is not the work of linguistics but, rather, a practical, concrete task which cannot be summarized as the task of transforming a whole culture, a society or a civilization. We have new signifiers, like 'fibre optics', 'nanosecond', 'market' and 'network'. But we just have an old word—'spirit'—to express what our words do not speak of, or not comprehensibly: How our existence— the existence of everyone, of all presences, human,

---

4 The supposed makers or trouble makers (*facteurs ou fauteurs*) of the degradation of these 'values' are also invoked: these are lowly counter-values like the 'selfishness' or 'greed' of businessmen, the 'cynicism' or 'hypocrisy' of producers/vendors, the taste for 'pleasure' or the 'voracity' of consumers/buyers, in short, a whole psychological and moral panorama— which too often psychoanalysis is alas used to reinforce—before which we remain pensive. Who has suddenly made so much individualism, infantilism, concupiscence and covetousness arise? What mean genie has corrupted humanity if not its own 'development'? These are pointless questions that more than one or two people try to answer . . .

living, cosmic—exists in the strong sense of the word, that is makes itself, forms itself, opens itself up to relationships . . .

We have the feeling, and even the awareness, that our civilization itself erased the spirit that had been its own. We cannot go backwards—or we paralyse existence.

Spirit today is already here, at least in this way: let us exist, desire and invent the forms, the meanings and the force to exist.

Inversely and *reciprocally*: When Marx speaks of the soul while thinking about the production by man of human value, he obviously knows that this value is neither a pure ideal floating in the air, nor a simple tangible reality like a piece of cloth or a rifle. He knows in fact that nothing exists in either of these forms which are both idealities of signification, words whose meaning makes sense only by being worked on, elaborated, transformed in usage and exchange for which there is no currency, no convertibility of values, no general equivalence. And that is what he can call, briefly, 'soul': the appropriation of what is not the property of anything but that is a self-property [*être-proprement*], an existing-in-and-of-itself [*proprement-exister*].

The *destruction of man by man* has always accompanied human production. Not just by war and murder but also by exploitation, subjection, domination, betrayal, theft and everything we can call 'alienation', whether it involves others or oneself. Alienation is in short correlated with the production of existence itself. It is so because this 'itself' [*propre*] is not given, not identifiable or able to be appropriated.

This is no small matter, and it has occupied people since there have been people. But a civilization that has become in itself, intrinsically, the domination by appropriation of all goods, on one hand, and which, on the other hand, has constructed the idol of a universal dominator who would reduce man to the role of executor of its domination—this civilization is in the process of unravelling and giving up on itself. Its spirit is entering into convulsion.

3

This spirit, though, is the spirit of what we still call 'emancipation': people's access to an independence from the forces of nature and from the oppression of some humans by others. Several times we have reached and crossed the thresholds of emancipation: from human sacrifices, from theocracies and hierarchies, from the integrated systems of royal or imperial administrations, from the apparatuses of Church and State. We were not on guard against the power of the mastery deployed both as engine and effect of this immense movement. This mastery over things, over the transformations of so-called raw materials and over the logics of production, has transformed all its agents into the subjected subjects of a great machine that we call 'economy' by laziness of language but that is actually not a separate sphere: it is the encompassing sphere of our own existence as humanity, as living beings throughout the universe. The *global* is indeed the name for a subjection in which we are madly struggling, calling for 'subjects' or 'subjectivations', which is to say, other oppositions and other wielders of another mastery . . .

One thing is certain: the 'spirit', whatever the inertia of this word may be,[5] at least points to what is not able to be assimilated or exploited. That which in effect doesn't stop resisting—resisting all oppressions, masteries, exploitations, persecutions—all subjections. It is absolutely not a matter of morality. It is a basic condition of the simple fact of existing. Existing, emerging from the self—emerging from any form of self per se, exposing oneself and being exposed: being in the element of meaning, to express it with a simple word.

Existence and meaning are not without what is opposed in them: that which by exposing itself seeks to impose itself, that which by opening meaning folds back in on itself. The secret of dominating conduct is never—this must always be repeated—that of a simple force. This force is asserted (even in its own eyes) as law, since it is already, necessarily, exercised on the level of meaning and not of pure mechanism. Of course there are tyrants who are simple tyrants. But the real 'politics' of all kinds of constructions of States, Empires, Chiefdoms are always those that open a system of meaning by trying to master it or else by placing this meaning in a way where it imposes itself by exposing itself. Force doesn't just make itself law, but law also means to impose itself. The impulse urges onward both desires together.

One could say, in traditional terms: the prophet cannot prophesy meaning unless he addresses the prince or even takes the prince's

---

5 And the traps it hides. See Jacques Derrida, *Of Spirit* (Geoffrey Bennington and Rachel Bowlby trans) (Chicago: University of Chicago Press, 1991).

place. The thought of a sense of universal equality and communication does not escape this law. It responds to the very energy of the spirit. It contains a considerable risk, but one that cannot be denied. We must 'make do with'. Which does not mean renounce the spirit.

Every great period of upheaval and loss of reference points rouses a spiritual energy. The collapse of ancient empires and the transformation of technologies allowed for the emergence of two cultures—Greek and Jewish. Rome's tribulation gave rise to Christianity. That of the Eastern empire gave rise to Islam. Maimonides appeared in a time of convulsions, Luther too . . . and Marx, and Heidegger. These figures of course are not the same, prophets sometimes dominating and sometimes dominated, sometimes lucid and sometimes blind (or both at once). But figures and names never form anything but visible signals. Each time, a breath passes through them that does not come from them. It comes from what we can call 'history', 'the people' . . . it comes from sufferings, rebellions, dreams, thoughts, desires, sometimes wanderings, curiosities, whims . . . It comes, in short, from this not-staying-the-same whose agents and patients 'we' are, by our existences.

Perhaps, moreover, we should talk less of History with a capital H—of that major process whose course carries everything and everyone along with it and to which a certain vision of divine promise, then human self-production, has habituated us—than of a pursuit of episodes during an adventurous course, made of meanderings and burrowings. Or else a sparkling constellation of contingencies, each one of which shines with a brief presence destined at once to nothing other than itself and to an elsewhere that cannot be located open to all, to their totality and to no one. After all, sense, in all the force of the word, is made of *that*: that energy, its fervour and its eclipses.

There are periods of vacation of the spirit. There are the 'Pax Romana's and 'Hundred Years' War'. Today we are in a particularly pronounced vacation, particularly sensitive in any case to what 40 years ago the Sex Pistols called the 'no future'. It is perhaps for this reason that the figure of the prophet has come to the forefront, while it vaticinates in every possible way: *New Age* (psychotropic) or Old Left ('responsibility!'), return to roots and to the frontiers ('sweet France').

The vacations of prophecy and energy always have surprises in store. That at least is not in doubt. The spirit blows where it likes. 'Paths of thought' lead to 'an *other* essence, *origin-heterogenous*' [*hétérogène à l'origine*].⁶ That is to say, it can arise only unexpectedly, impossible to identify and without any claims to establish, inaugurate or even begin. But a wind is rising, and in it, a desire. In desire, a decision, a determination to hold oneself ready for the unexpected. Better than a revolution: a resolution.

---

6 Derrida, *Of Spirit*, p. 107.

CODA

Here are some phrases written almost a century ago:

The force of events may drive and use us as much as it will, but by a little cunning, as it were, a little free will, if you like, we can still manage to keep our head above water. *We can recognize and understand the true inward direction of the process, and align ourselves with it consciously, not to the end of perpetuating the process, to be sure, but of consummating and fulfilling it within ourselves, and thus starting up the new process which is bound to ensue as the old has spent itself.* [...]

There is nothing to be solved today, but everything to be resolved; and the individual truly aware of how and where we stand knows this. Instinctively he pursues the path of the process rather than the formula. Instinctively he knows that all the dislocations today, the recurring crises, the injustices, wrongs, bloodshed, mean only one thing: that an old way of life has gone down never to rise again and that a new one is in the making precisely as the old spends itself.[1]

1 Michael Fraenkel, *The Michael Fraenkel: Henry Miller–Correspondence called 'Hamlet'*, VOL. I (London: Carrefour, 1962), from the letter dated

How slow life is
And how violent Hoping is.

---

26 May 1936, p. 165 (original emphasis) (with Jean-Luc Nancy's thanks to Marcia Cavalcante-Schuback). As for the lines by Apollinaire, from the poem 'Mirabeau Bridge' in *Alcools*, they were written in 1913.

A COMING WITHOUT PAST OR FUTURE

TRANSLATED BY

NIKOLAAS DEKETELAERE AND MARIE CHABBERT

1

We are often tempted today to perceive ourselves as a present devoid of a reliable past and future—'us' the inhabitants of so-called developed worlds that are shrouded each day a bit more by a fog in which the contours, meaning and direction [*sens*] of our advancement recede. Our past is of little help to us, whether it is the salvation of humanism or communism, and our future [*avenir*] gives us more doubts than assurances. We thus have a feeling of immobility or of hesitant suspension in which we find ourselves disoriented to the point of fleeing in what some call *presentism*. That term has a theoretical meaning (the affirmation of the exclusive existence of the present) as well as a practical one ('let us deal with the present, the rest is out of reach').

These attitudes are all ways of mourning [*porter le deuil*] history (a bereavement [*deuil*] announced for more than half a century). At least history understood as a relatively continuous process and relatively oriented towards a certain 'good life', to use Aristotle's expression that describes the stakes of communal life. The continuity bears itself out to be at least complex (the succession of techniques or ethics shows as many ruptures as linkages) and the

Lecture delivered at the conference 'Thinking with Jean-Luc Nancy', organized in Oxford in March 2019 by Marie Chabbert and Nikolaas Deketelaere.

orientation frankly doubtful when each new way of mastering is coupled with a new threat (for example, longevity coupled with fragility).

Mourning history, we do it badly and with difficulty. Our entire civilization has been innervated with a teleology that Nietzsche already suspected of masking the fractures of history. However, we do not know how to think these fractures, and the endeavours to set history off again through new myths have cost us dearly.

In a sense I am, without presentism, convinced of the importance of cultivating the present, of receiving its present (the gift) as allogeneic to time and as what Rimbaud calls 'eternity found again'.[1] However, I must make sure not to confuse eternity with sempiternity (the scholastics did this very well). It is not a matter of placing oneself in the present. Its gift is not the gift of stance, of stability, or of stele. Perhaps it even withdraws in its givenness, like the present essentially withdraws itself in the coming about [*advenue*] of its own succession. In succeeding, it passes, and in passing it opens itself to succeeding further. In so doing, it comes about [*s'advient*] by losing itself, it is received as what cannot be anticipated because it comes [*vient*]. In a word, it is not a future [*futur*]. The future is a present represented as certain or possible. (I allude, of course, to an idea that is very present and insistent in Derrida.) The coming-to [*l'à-venir*], to put it like that, would then be the pre-sence of the present, what does not take place yet and therefore

---

1 See 'Eternity' (May 1872) in Arthur Rimbaud, *Collected Poems* (Martin Sorrell trans.) (Oxford: Oxford University Press, 2001), pp. 181–3.—Trans

is not (it is only in our expectations, our fears, our calculations). It is thus not within the realm of the possible—or the impossible: it is not, and in not-being it exposes us to an absence or a void of which the approaching [*l'approche*] and the happening [*la survenue*] alone will give us the fugitive present.

Our present condition is thus not at all exceptional. It is the temporal condition, and only a particular form of projection has been able to make us anticipate futures [*futurs*] that are programmed, anticipated, and therefore present before being. We have known for a long time now that the forecasts of science-fiction, and more than one scientific forecast, have not turned out as anticipated. This does not impede anticipations from showing flair, sensitivity to forces and forms in the process of presenting oneself. Neither does it impede programmes from realizing themselves perfectly (like the atomic bomb or the moon landing), precisely because programming consists in making present to oneself everything that can be calculated, measured, evaluated—including hazards and risks. Neither has it ever prevented the failure of a programme (a shuttle that explodes) nor unanticipated consequences (voluntarily or not), for example Hiroshima, in its effects that are as much real as symbolic.

2

It is therefore necessary to free ourselves from mourning as well as from the representation we mourn: mastered history. Such is the ambivalence of the term *Anthropocene*: if it designates the substitution of man for natural forces, it can be understood (at least partially); but if it claims to hail a mastery and autonomy (not to say autocracy) of man, it represses the enormous uncertainty, or maybe even the misguidance, in which this mastery engages itself [*s'engage*] (and already begins to know itself bound [*engagée*] . . . and anxious).

Hence why I want to talk about a coming [*avenir*] without past or future [*futur*]. That is to say, to connect this to what I have just said, of the approach and the coming about of a void and an unknown whose past, or future, can wade off the emergence [*le surgissement*].

The emergence is nothing new in history, or in prehistory. After all, the world is an emergence: not only does it emerge from the non-world, but it also does not cease to emerge to itself, from energies to blasts, from assemblies to explosions, from molecules to cells and from cells to brontosauruses, quadrupeds, hominids, ziggurats and steam engines. Never has the precedent seen coming what follows. The space-time of the world—indeed, of plural worlds—is, fundamentally [*à son fond*], nothing other than emergence, even if it is indefinitely older than any age.

This also means that beginning and end are inherent, consubstantial to space-time, that is to say, to the distention and the expansion of the Thing, that is to say, of the real or of the nothing ex-istent.

I do not wish to venture here into the silence of the outside with which the Thing surrounds itself from as soon as it emerges [*surgit*]. Many myths and many physics have dedicated themselves to this splendidly for a long time. Many poets, also, like Octavio Paz, speak of

the face of being,
the void,
the fixed featureless splendour.[2]

Now, I would only like to let resonate for us something of this splendour and this silence: we should understand that, instead of wanting to detect and decipher the messages of the origin and end, we must make ourselves accustomed to the silence and obscurity that are at the heart of all jolting and emergence—be they shocks of particles, of the birth and death of the living, of our meditations or our delusions.

What Clarice Lispector, in a dizzying short cut, calls *the creative unconscious of the world.*[3]

For the Real or Nothing does not precede or follow the world, for space-time is not immersed in another space-time. It is the only one, however multiple it may be and however teeming its aspects and narratives. There is thus no outside—there is no outside if not inside, in the utmost intimacy, where there is emerging, bending, cracking, breaking-apart or conjoining.

---

2 Octavio Paz, *A Tale of Two Gardens: Poems from India, 1952–1995* (Eliot Weinberger trans.) (New York: New Directions, 1997), p. 87 (translation modified).

3 Nancy does not give the reference, but Lispector uses this phrase in her *The Stream of Life* (Elizabeth Lowe and Earl Fitz trans., Hélène Cixous Foreword) (Minneapolis: University of Minnesota Press, 1989), p. 70.—Trans.

This all seems very metaphysical and emphatic, it's true. However, it is in fact a matter of what exceeds all metaphysics and emphasis—all consideration and all discourse—what makes us open our eyes and speak.

The paradox could not be more logical: it is when we experience the harshest jolt that distance must be taken, a time marked. It is even, actually, what the jolt imposes on us and proposes to us. The history of progress has come to its completion, another history started within that completion. We cannot make it out. We must watch its invisibility, for it is within it that it comes. Which means that it has already begun, unbeknownst to us, and that it will not become identifiable but when it has already entered an advanced age.

Kant himself, at the height of his confidence in a rational history of which he saw the sign in the emergence of the Enlightenment, knew that he could not project a fulfilment of this history other than in a coming [*avenir*] so remote that he was very close to thinking it asymptotically. As it happens, it is precisely rational history or historical reason that eclipses itself before us. That is how it is to come [*à venir*] without past or future [*futur*].

3

Nothing in history reproduces itself. However, the novelty of a jolt or a rupture involves at least the formal analogy of eclipse and shock (perhaps each time a brief exposition to *the fixed featureless splendour*). What I call *formal* here is in truth of the order of affect, of upheaval, of trauma. We are in the register of birth and death, of the dazzling glare and the eclipsing of sight, of appearing and disappearing—this register has no history: it propels it. In that sense, there is no past, no tradition to revive without the tradition itself being subverted.

Nothing seems more striking to me than this: the West is put in question, and puts itself in question in all possible ways and under all possible angles (capitalism, progress, technology, democracy, atheism, *jouissance*, domination, etc.). The West, this name, even though it is so broad—so broad that it is broadly deterritorialized on the surface of the earth and even outside of it—continues to be, first of all, identified with certain territories. First of all, of course, Europe—even if it is flanked by its enormous American outgrowth. This denomination is not a mistake: there was once a Western jolt, whose first hold was Mediterranean. From this jolt, it is not a matter of fantasizing that a destiny put itself in motion, no more than a teleology of some kind that we may imagine. However, it is unquestionable that a sequence put itself in motion that carried within itself, in its genetic engineering, a distinctive trait of the mastery of time. While other civilizations envelop time in a permanence, this one [the West] has triggered a mastery of succession. A culture of duration [*la durée*]—then of progression—differs in kind from a culture of permanence. When a Roman poet—Horace—declares that he has *erected a monument more durable than bronze*,[4] one must understand how much the emphasis is put on the erection, on the working-out [*elaboration*]

4 Horace, *Odes*, 3.30.1–4.—Trans.

of the work [*l'œuvre*]. The operation prevails in the work, the enterprise in the monument.

Enterprise: it is a term that lends itself to emblematizing an important, if not essential, feature of the West. The true emergence of this feature occurs in Rome. Rome has all the features of an enterprise: it sets itself a project, which is its own production and exportation, or its extension. It manages this project consistently and through a set of related registers: a city-state that is original and shapes itself into an autarky, such that it becomes in fact a kind of civil religion, unknown even to the Greeks, and a moral identity (virtue), more so than a territorial or familial one; the elaboration of the first legal system conceived as a complete edifice in continuous construction; the development of a set of techniques (urban, military, agricultural, mechanical), unprecedented by its quasi-systematicity, many of which will subsequently take centuries to be rediscovered; and, finally, an expansion that is also unprecedented because it destroyed few cities (Carthage, first of all), rather including a great number of other ones that it allowed to subsist in the shadow of its strength and its law. It is Rome that invented the model of Empire in the sense that Europe will often seek to reprise: the autocratic domination of a diverse set of popular, cultural or religious units.

Rome does not merely take over the autonomy of Athens, it detaches it completely from the local and popular identity and opens it unto an enterprise that for the first time merits, on its scale, the name of globalization [*mondialisation*]. (One could add, if one wants to halt there, a comparison with the Chinese empire which, in a roughly neighbouring period, unified a vast expanse of territories according to quite a different dynamic, which one could call hoarding rather than enterprise.)

As we know, Rome collapsed. It is not by chance that Europe has kept the memory of this fall, which seemed so astonishing, so alive. Rome collapsed in on itself under its own weight: under the weight of an incapacity to find the meaning and direction [*sens*] of its own enterprise. As is known, fevers and philosophical and religious anxieties never ceased to stir, from two centuries before our era. When Constantine sought to revive the Empire by devoting it to Christianity, it was already too late.

4

For Christianity, this offshoot of a Jewish base, actually appeared as an attempted answer to the trouble of Rome. I believe that clear evidence of this is given by the behaviour of nascent Judaeo-Christianity towards wealth [*la richesse*]. This is well known, but we do not sufficiently ask ourselves what this means. The critique of wealth had been initiated by the philosophers and the Jews—which is telling. With Rome, however, one may think that what manifested itself much more decidedly was the substitution of what I would call *a wealth that exists in its deployment* [*richesse d'usage*], for what I would call *a wealth that brings glory*. I mean a wealth that is employed for revenue-oriented operations (trade, construction, etc.) in opposition to a wealth that is accumulated for the glory of its holder—for example, the gold and finery of a Pharaoh, or the gold that covers the Biblical Ark. I use the word *glory* to evoke what that notion holds sacred. I use the word *deployment* [*usage*] to turn away somewhat from a too-simple opposition between use-value and exchange-value. It is a question of grasping this: Rome (preceded, really, by others like Byblos, Tyre, Athens, Carthage, etc.) has been the hearth of a mutation of technology, domination and wealth—a mutation in which the long gestation of the West plays itself out.

Christianity is at once its product, symptom and intensification. It is its product because it mingles within itself the great aspirations that have been at work for centuries in the effacement of sacred worlds: the Greek autonomy of a *logos*, the Jewish alliance with a wholly-other, the energies issuing from the entire Eastern Mediterranean, from Egypt and the Etruscans. A powerful catalysis takes place there from which a new culture of mastery and enterprise, of project and emancipation, emerges. Christianity is its double symptom: on the one hand, it moves power out of the world, situating glory and fulfilment in another realm [*royaume*]—thus testifying to a congestion of the terrestrial realm [*royaume*]; and, on the other, by inviting man [*l'homme*] to renew himself, it opens up to him a freedom that is no longer of status but of activity: the new man is a task to be undertaken [*à entreprendre*]. In that sense, Christianity at the same time diverts and galvanizes the energetic, productive drive, brought about by the Roman mutation.

This does not immediately produce all of its effects; detours as long as those that preceded the Roman Empire are also needed. However, when the mutation that commits [*engage*] modern Europe instigates itself [*s'engage*], we find the threefold character of technology, domination and wealth, within the increased complexity of Christianity, that at the same time installed itself as terrestrial power and thus finds itself obliged to call itself into question and thus to displace itself (if not to deconstruct itself)—as it is still doing.

I will return later to the complexity thus designated. For the moment, I conclude with the birth of what in six or seven centuries has become the West. (Here I skirt the part of Islam in this history, first a notable participant in the enterprise and then turning away from it in favour of another history.)

Around the fourteenth century, the sequencing proper to the Western enterprise was fully underway: technology, domination and wealth fall under the same principle of momentum and expansion. What is called *capitalism* represents the systematic development of this principle, whose name could be *investment* [*l'investissement*]. 'To invest' is to surround, to envelop, to dress (vesting), a particular object in order to appropriate it. Technology vests a particular operation (transporting, drilling, etc.); domination vests the exercise of mastery (over people, goods, techniques); wealth—here it tends to be that of deployment only—vests the growth of its own capacity to invest itself (thanks to and in view of all kinds of technology and domination).

It will soon be a century since Valéry, at the time of the Second World War, wrote: 'Europe completes an astonishing, glittering and deplorable career, bequeathing to the world [. . .] the gloomy gift of positive Science and the sad example of the primacy of wealth, which had nowhere been seen so absolutely grounded in mores and in all things.'[5] By 'positive science,' Valéry means, as he says elsewhere, science as 'power—that is to say, formula or recipe for action', what has been coined as *technoscience* and can simply be called *technology*. As for wealth, Valéry is neither a Christian social-ist nor a communist; his judgement is all the more striking. It suf-fices to add the conjunction between science and wealth he makes a little further on: 'The power of action has conquered the domain of knowledge [. . . , and] with it its practical equivalent, *wealth*, and all the proteinic properties of it.'[6]

We can merely add this, which did not yet have a manifest character for Valéry: one of the proteinic properties of wealth is to transform, on the one hand, the social relations to the point of pushing most people into destitution while reserving an evermore insolent and powerful opulence for a minority that is evermore reduced; on the other, the subsistence relations between man and the rest of the world in a paralysis that is such that subsistence exhausts itself in it.

5

What exhausts itself is the West itself. This affirmation, to repeat it once more, is in no way a fated or teleological outlook: the sequencing of Western sequences obeys an investment of which the limit can consist only in a loss of the very possibilities of invest-ing. It could be that this is what is happening to us. However, it would then not only be a matter of energetic limits—whether this

5 Paul Valéry, *Cahiers*, II (Paris: Gallimard, 1974), p. 1533.
6 Valéry, *Cahiers*, Book 2, p. 1352.

is motor energy, the appetite for domination, or exponential enrichment. If any one of these registers, or more surely the braid of the three put together, knows a serious collapse [*affaisement*], it will only be to the extent that the investment underpinning the ensemble starts to subside [*s'affaisser*]: that of an unlimited power, that is to say, of which the investment consists in its own exercise.

Against the horizon of an indefinite expansion of technology and its domination, it is indeed no longer a question of being, as Descartes would have liked, 'master and possessor of nature'; it is rather a question of indefinitely enjoying or coming-to oneself [*jouir indéfiniment de soi*] (a bit like the Hegelian spirit), which, to (un)end, just as well boils down to its own exhaustive exhaustion. It is not a question of man, but of a self-sufficiency equal to its self-exhaustion.

One is irresistibly tempted to protest that it is inconceivable for man to disappear—and perhaps with him life and nature—in nearing the limit of his own power. Why would that not be conceivable? The question can be asked. It is not obvious that the value we deem to attribute to man—and even the one we think we attribute to life—is a value, that is to say, a sense worthy of the name. It may be precisely that, if the sense of man and that of life were given by man himself or by life itself, they would remain far removed from that which wills an infinite sense! Hans Jonas asserts that our responsibility is to ensure 'the permanence of an authentically human life on earth.'[7] The term 'authentically' harbours a

----

7 Hans Jonas, *The Imperative of Responsibility: In Search of an Ethics for the Technological Age* (Hans Jonas and David Herr trans) (Chicago: University of Chicago Press, 1984), p. 11 (translation modified). Elisabeth

problem that paralyses the very idea of such a responsibility from the outset.

It is impossible for us to decide in favour of an authenticity of which nothing tells us the content—or else of which everything, on the contrary, could invite us to consider that this content lies precisely in the indefinite deployment of the autonomous power of which man would have been the vector for the entirety of the world. What if the authentic man were the one by whom the supreme blaze and extinction of the 'creative unconscious' accomplishes itself?

Being sensitive to the Heideggerian motif of the *Brauch* of man by being is not excluded: of the *use* of man by his own ex-istence—thus of the use [*usage*] of deployment [*usage*] itself, of its utilization, of its utility and wear [*usure*] as the wearing-out [*usure*] of sense itself. Because, after all, the meaning does not have to be interminable. It is rather infinite each time in the truth of its interruption: in an encounter, in a culture, in a work, in an existence. In that

de Fontenay has, already more than 20 years ago, very well formulated that which prevents us from referring ourselves to an authenticity: 'The lack of criteria enjoins us to respond in the absence of any referentiality, to keep this empty exigency that precedes the subject and exceeds all authority' ('Quelque chose comme du donné . . .' in *La responsabilité*, Paris: Autrement, 1994). [Nancy cites *Le Principe responsabilité* (Paris: Cerf, 1990), Jean Greisch's 1990 translation of Jonas' *Das Prinzip Verantwortung* (Frankfurt am Mein: Insel Verlag, 1979), that renders Jonas' principle as 'assurer la permanence d'une vie authentiquement humaine sur terre' (p. 31), where the German speaks of an 'echten menslichen Lebens auf Erden' (p. 36). For clarity, we have stuck to the French rendering in our English translation of Nancy's text.—Trans] sense, it is interminable because it can always be interrupted and sets itself off again in its own interruption (all the questions of the 'work' tie themselves together at this point).

6

What revolts us is the ignominy of an injustice and a denial of humanity in the irresistible deployment of power. There is no resistance to this irresistibility that does not have to, if it is to resist, put what we believe to be able to call *the authenticity of human life* back into play. Returning to the beginning of my remarks, I would say: just like the congestion and anxiety of Rome triggered Christianity in all its ambivalence, so too is it not impossible that the congestion and anxiety of our times—lasting for more than a century— triggers a jolt, it too unforeseen and unidentifiable, it too carrying a line of flight compared to the sequencing in which we feel ourselves to be caught up.

The important thing is that this jolt can only be like what Marx calls 'the spirit' when he castigates religion (but with it, fundamentally, everything that pretends to give a sense of the world) as 'the spirit of a spiritless world'.[8] What does that word spirit [*esprit*] mean? This is certainly what always emerges unexpectedly and without identity. This is certainly what is without past and without future [*future*]—like the Son of God or the autonomous

---

8 Karl Marx, *Critique of Hegel's 'Philosophy of Right'* (Annette Jolin and Joseph O'Malley trans) (Cambridge: Cambridge University Press, 1870), p. 131 (translation modified).—Trans

Man. And if our time tests us [*nous éprouve*] with its injustice deprived of any horizon, it is sure that the spirit to come [*l'esprit à venir*] is that of a justice, that no adjustment, no reform of the conditions of today, can bring into view.

I will allow myself to quote a few lines written 17 years ago. Less to prevail in having anticipated anything than simply to show that which comes across us and beckons us, perhaps already for some time. It was in a book whose title (*The Creation of the World, or Globalization*) wanted to mark a sharp contrast between emergence [*surgissement*] and transformation, between mutation and modification. Here it is:

> *To create the world* means: immediately, without delay, reopening each possible struggle for a world, that is, for what must from the contrary of a global injustice against the background of general equivalence. But this means to conduct this struggle precisely in the name of the fact that this *world* is coming out of nothing, that there is nothing before it and that it is without models, without principle and without given end, and that is precisely *what* forms the justice and the meaning of a world.[9]

What is unprecedented and perhaps comes about [*advient*] without past or future [*futur*], is the escape from all terminal signification. It is the sense of the fact that we have no mastery over our ends,

---

9 Jean-Luc Nancy, *The Creation of the World, or Globalization* (François Raffoul and David Pettigrew trans) (Albany: SUNY Press, 2007), pp. 54–5.

and that they are not our masters either, for all of this falls under logics of investment and deployment in view of an interminable revival of power, both productive and destructive. We have no mastery over the sense of the world, but perhaps we are ourselves not mastered by the power either, if we are instead employed (*gebraucht*), utilized, put in play by no master, by no signification but our simple putting into play. Our existence according to the presence that comes and that comes to us might be what exists only by and for itself, for its own fruition (I am alluding here to the *frui* of Augustine, to the 'enjoyment' or 'coming' [*jouir*] that Heidegger links with his *gebrauchtsein*. Not 'enjoying oneself' or 'coming-to-oneself' [*jouir de soi*] like the Hegelian spirit, but being enjoyed [*être joui*] . . .).

Here, now, I am employed, utilized, demanded, exploited, enjoyed [*joui*] by an infinite that is neither subject nor a plan—which therefore destines me to nothing and derives no profit from me—but that is my very existence, the fact that it is sent, dispatched to its only effectiveness of being—this body, these words, this thrust, this chance insofar as they are here and now exposed, devoted, abandoned to infinitely more than them.

This is not an easy thought and it isn't a thought at all: it is a *praxis*, an *ethos*, a lived and living disposition with which, in a sense, we are already familiar without even knowing it. For it is not an object of knowledge. It is rather the fact of a jolt, of a gap as regards the using [*usagière*] and wearing-out [*usante*] logic that exhausts us. A disjunction, a putting-out-of-order—as much as a divine surprise.

111